"One God . . . Three Gods?" is the book of the film. The ITV network series, produced and directed by Jeffrey Milland, over six weeks of the summer of 1986 sets out to present and provoke. Is there scope for dialogue between three step-cousins – Judaism, Christianity and Islam?

Christopher Martin, a Church of England priest who earns his living in the world of the media, was before his ordination for sixteen years Religious Broadcasting Officer of the IBA. From that post, he had many opportunities to recognize in Jeffrey Milland, a Jew, one of the most talented and perceptive religious television makers of our day.

The opportunity to collaborate on this project marks the fruit of many years conversation and friendship. So Christopher Martin went to Jerusalem to set up the series, and with Gillian Reynolds as the experienced reporter, the HTV team followed in his footsteps.

This book unfolds the creation of a television series that is bound to challenge comfortable presuppositions, and make its contribution towards dialogue between the three monotheistic religions that between them colour our lives and our common culture.

ONE GOD... THREE GODS?

by
CHRISTOPHER MARTIN

with a
Foreword
by
Donald Coggan
formerly Archbishop of Canterbury

CHURCHMAN PUBLISHING
1986

ONE GOD . . . THREE GODS?
was first published in 1986 by

CHURCHMAN PUBLISHING LIMITED
117 Broomfield Avenue
Worthing
West Sussex
BN14 7SF

and distributed to the book trade by

BAILEY BROS. & SWINFEN LIMITED
Warner House
Folkestone
Kent
CT19 6PH

Churchman's agents in Canada
Jonathan Gould Books of Winnipeg

© Copyright Christopher Martin and HTV Limited

All rights reserved

ISBN 1 85093 038 4

Printed in Great Britain by Whitstable Litho Limited

Foreword
by
Donald Coggan
formerly Archbishop of Canterbury

The aim of this book (which is the aim of the film behind it) is "to explore where the three faiths – Judaism, Christianity and Islam overlap, particularly through the experiences of those who have been touched by more than one of them." As such, the book is to be welcomed.

There will be plenty of points within it which adherents of any one of the three faiths will disagree – the field is immense and any attempt to deal with it must employ shorthand language. But that is beside the mark. In this book situations are sketched; characters are depicted; the tangle of problems is presented; and when we are almost at our wits' end, our relief comes through laughter.

This is not primarily a book for experts in comparative religion. The problems with which it deals are on the doorsteps not only of those who live in the Middle East but on *our* doorsteps – for life at the end of the twentieth century is lived in one great international mix, and at the heart of the mix is religious belief.

Down the centuries we have all mishandled the problems, and the results have been catastrophic. May this book help us all to do better as the twenty-first century approaches.

Donald Coggan

(Lord Coggan is Executive Chairman of the Council of Christians and Jews)

1
One God . . . Three Gods?

"Excuse me, I am looking for the Christian Embassy."

Teeth click, and there is a nod of incomprehension. Jerusalem, and it is towards nightfall on a wet Thursday in March. At their muddy station just east of no man's land, Arab buses fill, their old engines roaring, ready to disperse before curfew to the Palestinian enclaves.

"Excuse me . . ." My next appointment is in West Jerusalem, to visit an Orthodox rabbi in his apartment in the select suburb of Rehavia. All I can remember is that he lives opposite the Christian Embassy. He mentioned this as a landmark, and a joke. The creation of American conservative Christians, who uncritically support the state of Israel, it cuts no ice with its neighbours. It is no use my trying to check the rabbi's address in a telephone directory. Any publicly available directories in East Jerusalem are in Arabic, which I cannot read. I can just pick out the letters of someone's name in Hebrew, but Hebrew directories are to be found only in West Jerusalem, where they are plentiful. There are even ones there in English, but they are rather out of date.

"Excuse me . . ." but it is unthinkable to enquire of the passing Chassidim. They keep themselves strictly to themselves, this black-clad remnant of expectant Jewry.

Oblivious of all the panoply of Israeli occupation, they walk to their place of prayer protected against the rain. Their broad-brimmed low-crowned hats are swathed in polythene, and down the sides of their faces their ringlets of hair swing without getting wet. But then they are carrying umbrellas, and the drops of rain drip off on to the skullcaps of their shaven-headed sons.

"Excuse me . . ." This looks more hopeful. Here by the entrance to the Garden Tomb somebody should surely be able to direct me to the Christian Embassy. For it is the site that a century ago General Gordon of Khartoum identified as the place of Jesus' burial. Since then it has nicely served Protestants who do not feel at home in the overladen traditional shrine, the Church of the Holy Sepulchre.

"I am sorry," comes in reply that unmistakable Swedish singsong.

"I am a stranger here myself." There is nothing for it but to enquire at a tourist office. They are bound to know. The two men and a woman behind the counter abandon their genuine customers while they consider the question. Could it be Terra Sancta, the office of the Franciscans who for the past 750 years have guarded the Christian holy sites? No. Or the Pontifical Institute? No. They are baffled. Then one of them produces an English language telephone directory, and there is the answer. I am half an hour late for my appointment with the Orthodox rabbi.

★ ★ ★

Religion, religion, religion! Jerusalem is full of it. The various brands and traditions jostle and crowd and compete. It would be the ideal city, a cynic suggested, for starting a school of militant atheism.

It is full of it. It is full of them. For the three related monotheistic religions – Judaism, Christianity, Islam, it is a holy city. From across the world, Jahweh, Abba, Allah draw their faithful here. One God, three Gods. For centuries a few careful scholars have studied the relationships between the three religions. Only now does there begin to emerge a wider concern to open them a little to each other.

The past is full of enmity, sprinkled with toleration. Springing out of Judaism, Christianity soon claimed to be worldwide in its appeal. In Jesus Christ, ran the message of the early apostles, God had shown himself to all men. The gospels and the rest of the New Testament were written not only in the light of what happened at Easter. They were largely written, and certainly compiled, in the lurid afterglow of the sack of Jerusalem. What clearer evidence could there be that the god of the universe had completed the mission of his ancient people the Jews, and now his salvation was on offer to all men?

But the Jews, scattered as they were, did not adopt the new

faith that had sprung from their loins. They clung on for grim death to their old religion. So they endured long centuries of Christian disdain and persecution that culminated in our own day with the horror of the Nazi final solution.

Elsewhere the Jews fared generally somewhat better. For after the sack of Jerusalem they also scattered east and south beyond the rule of Rome and its Christian heirs. They were at home in the cities of the wide desert world that from the seventh century of our common era fell under the sway of Islam. The religion of God's final revelation though his prophet Mohammed (blessed be his name) spread like wildfire from Mecca. Westwards it spread across North Africa, and, except in Egypt, soon stifled the Christian Church. It spread into Spain, and under its lee the Jews spread with it. Northwards it swept through Asia Minor, again extinguishing those first gentile churches that Paul and his companions had planted. Only in the Levant itself did Christian and Jew co-exist under the sign of the crescent as it cut its way eastwards, in a different form, to the lands around the Persian Gulf and beyond.

By the year 1000 the boundaries were established for the long clash between Christendom and Islam. They were the two world religions, rivals to the death. Crusade followed crusade, with the goal of recovering Jerusalem as the heart of the Christian world. Not until the close of the fifteenth century could Christian Europe be assured of its superiority. For though in 1453 Constantinople fell, and under the Ottomans Islam established its bridgehead on the soil of Europe, and for three more centuries threatened its Hapsburg heart, the threat was contained. For within twenty years of the fall of Constantine's city, Vasco de Gama had found the sea route round Africa, and Islam was encircled.

The Jews, who in Christian Europe were constantly at risk, in the lands under Muslim sway fared generally better. They were *Dhimmi* – aliens – certainly, but generally they were tolerated, and in many parts of that Arab world, particularly in Egypt, numbers of them rose to positions of influence and prominence. In their dispersion they had also spread beyond the reach of Islam. Even now the Falasha of Ethiopia, newly restored to Israel, are fighting to prove the authenticity of their Jewishness. In India, now, over a million Jews of ancient descent await encouragement to return to the land of their origin.

So, in barest outline, the scene is set. One god, three gods: our business is to report on where the three faiths touch and overlap today, particularly through the experiences of those, in and around Jerusalem, who have been touched by more than one of them.

For Jews, Christians and Muslims are cousins. They have not evolved an understanding of one supreme God of the universe independently. They have inherited and developed it from one another. They all look back to Abraham as their founding father. They all regard the character of this god of theirs as revealed, in successive relations. Theirs is not a god, they claim, of human imagination or reason. The list of those through whom revelation has come begins in common: Abraham, Moses and Elijah are revered by all three. Christians complete the list by Jesus of Nazareth as the Christ; Muslims also hold him in the highest honour, and the son of Mary; and then add Mohammed (blessed be his name) as the bearer of the final revelation.

Nor is there between Jews, Christians and Muslims any disagreement about the oneness of God. Given our title 'One God, Three Gods?', some of those to whom we spoke thought we were seeking to contrast the unitarianism of Judaism and Islam with the Christian doctrine of the Trinity. Some Christians, hearing the title, expressed shock. Were we out on a limb, claiming three Christian gods against others' one? Rather than wrestling with the forgotten acrostics of the Athanasian creed, we explained instead that our title was meant to be arresting. If they preferred to think of it as 'One God . . . Three Religions', they could do so.

Moreover, the distinction between the Christian Trinity and the one god of the Jews and the Muslims is not so absolute as it seems. In the traditional Hebrew formula the unnameable god is the God of Abraham, the God of Isaac and the God of Jacob: the threefold formula is there. It is not too fanciful to see it as the forerunner of the Christian formula. The God of Abraham is the creator, the begetter of the nation; the God of Isaac is the one who was prepared to be sacrificed; the God of Jacob is the one who wrestled all night to win the promise of life for himself and his heirs.

Even Islam has traces of a threefold understanding of god, despite its militant rejection of Trinity. God the supreme creator is all-merciful, and also judge. There are traditionally 99 names for God (three times three times eleven) and the camel is happy because he knows the hundredth.

For the Christian it is normal to begin praying by calling on the name of the Father, the Son and the Holy Spirit. To do so in Jerusalem feels a defiant gesture. A good nun offered her solution to the problem; "Begin by saying nothing". Even at the apparent point of their deepest disagreement, the three related religions have in common a belief in the oneness of god.

To say this is to say a very great deal. It goes most of the way towards establishing the kinship of the three religions. Completely separate religious traditions, such as that of the Zulus, or the Tao te Ching, in their own ways expressed a belief in the one universal power. Yet as against all other religious traditions that seek after one god, the most basic attributes to God in Judaism, Christianity and Islam are distinctive. God is creator sustainer, judge, and relates actively to the faithful.

Besides that, Jews, Christians and Muslims all see their god as totally good. So history has a purpose and an end. The world matters, and religion is to do with celebrating the everyday. Its business is to go on showing what God's good ends demand of human beings, together and alone.

How then, do the three religions relate to one another?

Jews and Muslims

The place to start is with Jews and Muslims, with people rather than isms and with the stories that tell their origins. Theirs is the oldest relationship. For though Islam is the youngest of the three religions, it looks straight back like the others to Abraham. For Muslims trace their descent from Abraham through his first born son, Ishmael, child of his slavegirl Hagar (Genesis 16, 11–12 records the poetic core of this ancient story). Abraham, we read, had despaired of God's promise that had brought him from the city of Ur to the uplands of Canaan. He was not content to let his heritage pass through his nephew Lot, who had chosed to settle in the fertile plain of the Dead Sea. His own wife, Sarai, was barren. So he took matters into his own hands and by Hagar fathered Ishmael. But Sarai would have none of this, and drove Hagar out. Thus her son became "the wild ass of the desert, his hand against everyman and everyman's hand against him."

The narrative brings Ishmael back, to be circumcised by Abraham, but then he and his mother are in the desert again, dying of thirst. There the angel of the Lord finds them water, and promises Ishmael that the Lord will make of him a great nation.

Meanwhile God fulfils his promise to Abraham, and against all natural expectation his wife, now Sarah ("princess") produces him a legitimate heir, Isaac. The greatest test comes when Abraham feels called to go and sacrifice Isaac to the Lord. In the nick of time an angel stays his hand, and there is a ram caught in a thicket to serve as the beast of sacrifice.

In the next generation the story repeats itself. Isaac's wife Rebecca produces twins, Esau the elder, Jacob the younger. But by hard bargaining Jacob robs Esau of his birthright, and then by trickery, with his mother's help, of his father's dying blessing to his older son. All that Isaac has left to promise Esau is that in time he will free himself from his supplanting brother's yoke.

These stories still run deep, and have much to say about how Jews and Muslims see themselves and one another. To the Jews they are constant reminders of God's faithfulness and promise against all the odds, provided only that his people remain faithful to him. Built in with that is the recognition that they survive and succeed largely by their own efforts. They are a reminder too that in the land of promise they will always be at odds with those around them.

Muslims look to Ishmael as their source of descent from Abraham. They do not so regard Esau, since he is the son of Isaac, the child of promise. Yet the two stories clearly reinforce one another, and speak of long established rivalry between the related peoples.

Until the beginning of this century, that rivalry was muted. Across the Islamic world, Jews from generation to generation sustained themselves as a minority. There was always pressure upon them, and a constant trickle of apostasy as individuals found it convenient to abandon their awkward religion. The promises of Genesis seemed hardly to be fulfilled. Ishmael's descendants, indeed Esau's, were keeping the upper hand. Yet the God of Abraham, of Isaac and of Jacob was a faithful god. Had he not, after four hundred years, through his servant Moses, brought his people out of slavery in Egypt? Had he not, in the 6th century BC, within a lifetime restored his people from exile in Babylon? He took his time, and was not above punishing his people for their sins, but to those who remained faithful to him, his promises were sure.

To the faithful Jew, the survival of his race over four thousand years of persecution and exile is the living proof of God's mercy. Other peoples rise and fall; the Jew survives. With the Armenians as the only possible comparison, to Gentiles the continuance of Jewry is an astonishment; but there they are.

The beginning of this century saw the growth of the Zionist movement. After centuries when only handfuls of Jews remained in the holy land, came the drive to return. Within twenty years of the first Zionist Congress in 1896, the Balfour Declaration promised Jews after the war a national homeland in Palestine. Students of the scriptures even managed to find a prophecy fulfilled in Allenby's conquest of Jerusalem, and Zionism became a serious political force.

One effect it had was to disturb Muslim toleration of Jews living in their midst. Arab nationalism was also rampant, as the Ottoman Empire crumbled. In Turkey itself Ataturk sought to westernise his country, by introducing the Roman alphabet and encouraging a secular state. By contrast the Arabs sought new inspiration from their common language and the common religion that it enshrined. For a generation Islamic militancy was held in check, as from 1918–1948 the western powers maintained their hold over the middle east. Instead it sought its outlet in a revived hatred for the Jews as they began to colonise their holy land. The early kibbutzim, founded between the two world wars, retain the appearance of stockades set up in alien territory. But the Jews had their support. From all around the diaspora, already in those years, money began to pour in to swell the Jewish National Fund and buy up land from Palestinian Arabs ready to sell.

It is rash to identify with Islam Arab reaction to Jewish settlement. The mainthrust of Zionism was secular, the first opposition to it not so much religious as the simple fear of those whose land is threatened.

Yet embedded into Islam is the belief in *Jihad* – holy war. It was not a long step from opposition to *Jihad*. *Jihad* once justified aggression. Islam was a universal religion, and it was the duty of the faithful to fight for its spread. Muslim apologists now prefer to describe *Jihad* as defensive, the protection of the faith against aggressors. Jews colonising Palestine provided a perfect pretext for *Jihad*. At first it was held in check: the British mandate purported to keep the rivals apart. Clearly, with the Arab Legion as its local militia, British sympathies were with the Palestinians. Film of British forces refusing entry to unregistered Jews arriving by the boatload at Haifa in 1946 remain imprinted on the memory. *Jihad* had its allies.

The war of 1948 – "the War of Independence" ended in uneasy truce. No Arab state recognised the state of Israel. At the slightest sign of Israeli aggression the faithful were ready to drive the colonisers back into the sea. Ranged against them was a beleaguered minority equally determined to hang on to their tiny new state.

Nearly forty years later there is little modification in Muslim attitudes to the existence of the state of Israel. Following the Camp David accords of 1978, President Carter achieved his greatest diplomatic triumph in presiding over the rapprochement between Israel and Egypt. Menachim Begin, previously a leader of the freedom-fighting Irgun, along with President Sadat received the Nobel Peace Prize. In return for handing back the Sinai, conquered in the six day war of 1967, Israel at last had one Arab neighbour with whom it had peaceful relations.

Now the bus leaves daily from Jerusalem to Cairo, and Israelis suffering from confinement enjoy making the trip. There is less traffic the other way. Only a handful of Egyptian pilgrims visit the shrines. It is from further afield, for instance from northern Nigeria, that planeloads of Muslims come to the holy city, to visit the Dome of the Rock and the Al Aqsa mosque, that are the architectural glory of Jerusalem.

On that sacred site some measure of understanding between

the three faiths begins to emerge. Seated behind a desk, radiating sanctity, is sheikh Mohammed Said el-Jamal. He is a sufi, about fifty years old, his trim ginger beard emerging from his brimless headgear. "There is only one god," he says. "Moses is his prophet, Jesus is his prophet, Mohammed is his prophet, blessed be their names."

Christians and Jews

"Between Judaism and Christianity there can be no dialogue. Between Christians and Jews, perhaps." So declares Professor Yehoshyuha Leibowitz, 82-year old learned Jew. After nearly two thousand years of strained relations, dialogue between Christians and Jews is beginning to take place. The two related historical events – the "holocaust" and the founding of the state of Israel, in Jewish eyes determine the conversation. Christians, they maintain, cannot ignore these events. In the light of them they must take pains to revise their understanding of their religion.

Christians find it hard to deny these terms. They have a deep sense of collective guilt about the horrors of the extermination camps. Even though as individuals they may have no direct responsibility for what happened, and may in one way or another have fought against it, how do they deflect Jewish insistence that the "holocaust" is not just a Nazi crime but Christian Europe's darkest blot? For in Jewish eyes it cannot and will not be separated from centuries of Christian persecution. When President Reagan made his badly handled German tour to mark the fortieth anniversary of VE day, Christians were inviting Jews to offer some collective expression of forgiveness. The Jewish response was that this was impossible. Only God can forgive. Christians found this refusal hard to take. Surely we are all meant to forgive our persecutors. Jews were obdurate. For a few survivors now to say publicly, or even privately to their Christian friends, "we forgive you," does not, runs their argument, itself forgive a crime of such enormity.

Yet "holocaust" is a daunting word. It puts its own stamp on that massacre, insisting that by its sheer scale and brutality it is of a different order from any previous persecution. Demanding that it should determine how Christians see their relations with Jews underlines this distinction. Holocaust takes on the epic size of other cataclysms in the Jewish collective memory, alongside exodus and exile and diaspora. Christians have been ready enough, all along, to read a theological significance into the first two events. They are part of the scripture which Christians claim to be as much theirs as the Jews'.

Christians have long learned to make exodus theirs by reading from it the pattern of deliverance that Christ brings. They can make the collective memory of exile theirs too, by treating is as the recurring experience of being all cut off from God. It is still hard for them to find how to handle what the Jews insist on calling holocaust.

The one Christian attempt so far to do so came in 1972, when Pope Paul VI formally exonerated the Jews for collective responsibility for the execution of Jesus the Christ. Other Christian traditions might have considered themselves long exempt from the taint of that indictment. In Jewish eyes they were not. How deep and wide the scar runs amongst Christians can be seen by looking at the way scholars study the Gospel of St. John. For it in those pages that the Jews are most clearly singled out as responsible for Jesus' death, of which, as John alone records, Pilate washed his hands.

Generation after generation, John's gospel had given a spurious warrant for Christian anti-semitism. Only recently have scholars drawn much attention to the fact that what the Authorised Version (and most new ones) translates as "the Jews" is more correctly to be understood as the people of Judaea. Jesus and his disciples were men of Galilee, and not at home in the capital city. A careful reading of the relevant gospel passages makes it clear that John sees the inhabitants of Jerusalem and its environs as the opposition to this northern Jewish religious movement.

The other event which Jews insist determines any agenda of dialogue with Christians is the existence of the state of Israel. Forty years after its founding, and nearly twenty after the unification of the city of Jerusalem, to Jews the state's existence is the complement of the holocaust. Out of the pit of suffering came redemption. Again, therefore, Jews insist that Christians who want to discuss their two religions must see in the state of Israel something of more than passing political significance. Between 70CE and 1948CE it might have been possible for Christians to insist that they were the true heirs of Jewry, and treat those who refused the Messianic message as an obstinately enduring minority. Christians, Jews maintain, can no longer do so. They must somehow learn to take the existence of the state of Israel as a sign of God's continuing providence to his ancient people. It is therefore no longer possible, the argument runs, for Christians to treat Jews as potential converts.

For the state of Israel demonstrates God's favour to the Jews and in consequence Christians must modify their belief in their missionary task to convert the whole world.

It is one thing for well-meaning Christians to agree politely to these terms of dialogue. To take them as seriously as they are meant hurts much more. For while Judaism has never seen itself as out to convert the whole world, Christianity always has. Is it now to accept its forebears's insistence that it may no longer do so?

Issues such as these provide the frame for discussion in the meetings of minds at the Rainbow Club. Named after the sign that the Lord God gave to Noah after the flood, the Rainbow Club has chapters that meet in Jerusalem, in Paris, in New York and in London. Once a year the London chapter invites a few guests to share in the conversation. The meeting takes place, appropriately, in the Jerusalem Chamber of Westminster Abbey, for many years past under the co-chairmanship of the Dean of Westminster Edward Carpenter, and Rabbi Hugo Gryn of the West London Liberal Jewish synagogue.

Each year the meeting takes a particular theme, and invites a paper from a Christian and a Jew to set out the issues. For 1985 the subject was "mission". With Revd Marcus Braybrooke and Rabbi Jonathan Dagonet providing the introductory papers, the matter at issue was very clearly set out. Essentially Christians must believe in mission: theirs is a world faith, and their business is to convert the heathen. Jews, by contrast, are under no such compunction. To be faithful to their calling, their business is to survive, and to keep unblemished the law and the commandments. It is not for them to seek to make converts. Indeed it is hard to find anyone who, apart from considerations of marriage, has converted from any other faith, or from none, to Judaism.

Even a dialogue such as this soon finds its way into the kitchen. Other religions, including the different brands of Christianity, are increasingly tolerant of mixed marriages. Why this pressure on those marrying Jews to convert? Otherwise, comes the answer, they won't be able to eat together; how can a Gentile bride cook Kosher food?

Scholarly Christians wipe their brows in perplexity. Why, they wonder, won't these Jews be serious? Here we are met to discuss mission, and they can only talk about cooking. The Jews are unabashed. One of them quotes the old German saying "man ist was er isst" – man is what he eats – as if that settles the matter. We can talk about food, but what does it mean to talk theology?

There is revelation, yes, there is *Torah* – the law embedded in the first five books of the scriptures. After that it is all a matter of obedience, and of commentary. The notion of man finding out more about God by other means – "theology" – is not part of Jewish understanding.

Professor Leibowicz put it more succinctly. "For an observant Jew religion is about bed, board and work. Nothing else, no, not even worship." Jewish–Christian dialogue has a long way to go.

Christians and Muslims

Western Christian dialogue with Islam begins from other premises. "That Lord Mayor of Bradford," said the man in the pub, "is a Paki and he read from the Koran, in Yorkshire!" Everybody in the bar laughed but they didn't snigger or boo; it was a good humoured evening, and the village had had a successful day's cricket. But there was nervousness in the laughter. The tolerant English, sitting loose to their tolerant national church, do not quite know how to take the establishment amongst them of Islam. "There are more Muslims than Methodists," has been uttered so long that as a statistic it may no longer be adequate. Christians need to talk with Muslims before it is too late. If in England the number of practising Muslims came to match the number of practising Christians, what hope for dialogue then?

Not only in England, but across western Europe, Muslims have come to stay. They do not keep a low profile, as Jews have customarily done. Islam is a missionary religion.

Gai Eaton is an English convert to Islam. Despite a conventional public school upbringing, he managed to stay detached from the Christian faith as there presented. Instead, at the end of his teens, he developed an interest in comparative religion. His work took him shortly after the war to Egypt, where he felt at home in Muslim surroundings, but it was after that, in Jamaica, that he submitted to his new faith. He is an urbane and cultured gentleman, frequently invited to address Christian groups. "But our faiths are essentially the same," his audiences exclaim with relief at the end of his presentation. Patiently he insists that they are not. Essential to Muslim belief is the conviction that God cannot suffer. Essential to Christian belief is that he has, and does. Again, for Muslims, the concept of Paradise is in the forefront of faith; for Christians, in Gai Eaton's judgement, life after death is no longer very important. Challenged with the comment that these differences are most apparent in mainstream English Christianity today, and that the tradition as a whole would make less of them, Gai Eaton is unmoved. To him Islam is different, and a superior vehicle of truth.

His stand challenges the conventional western Christian picture of Islam. Arrantly, the Book of Common Prayer speaks of "Turks, Jews and infidels" and the Muslims are the latter. They are the faithless ones, who fought their way across much of the Christian world under the crescent-shaped shadow of the scimitar. When in the year 1099AD the dreaded Saladin ousted the Knights of St. John from their hold upon Jerusalem, the battle-line hardened. The infidel controlled the holy city, and the call of Christians was to drive him out. Nobody paused to examine and compare Christian and Muslim belief. They were enemies, and the Christian call was to fight.

Against this long background of the crusades, one missionary incident stands out in bright relief. In about the year 1220 the modest figure of Francis of Assisi appeared in the Sultan's camp in the Nile delta. The Sultan received him kindly and Francis set about seeking to convert him and his followers to the Christian faith. The Sultan was evidently moved by this humble man of God, and made sure that he went on his way peaceably. He did not change his religion.

Now Christians want to enter into dialogue with Muslims before it is too late. For centuries they have been content to dismiss Islam as inferior, even though for many centuries the lamp of learning shone brightest in the universities of the Arab world. Even now it is easy for Christians of the west to cry out in righteous indignation at the excesses of Islam. The regime of Ayatollah Houmeini in Iran, Idi Amin's tyranny in Uganda and Bokassa's in Central Africa have all been cruel and oppressive. Besides them, the Islamic Republic of Pakistan, and the new powers in the Sudan add to the catalogue of tyranny. Even in Egypt now there is growing pressure to restore the *Shari'a* – the rule of Muslim law – with all its oppression and narrowness. The very word Islam means submission, and what scope can there be for dialogue with Christians who claim to follow one "whose service is perfect freedom"?

All that is to look at Islam from the angle of western Christianity. In the Arab world itself Christians have for centuries been living side by side with Muslim majorities. In the Levant, in Egypt, in Ethiopia, and even in Mesopotamia, Christians have long learned to keep their faith warily intact. Now, in Israel itself, Christians and Muslims have common cause. They are both second class citizens in the Jewish Independent State, or in the territories which it governs.

There what matters to Christians and Muslims is that they are both Arabs, both Palestinians. Religion is subordinate, a precious matter of inheritance. In the same year (1972) that he formally absolved the Jews for responsibility for Jesus' death, Pope Paul VI established Bethlehem University. Using substantial Roman Catholic premises, he established a campus designed to attract Muslim as well as Christian students. Of the present student roll of 1500, somewhat more than half are Muslim, and Muslims enjoy a number of senior positions on the university staff.

The students mix freely together. The groups of young men and young women who congregate to gossip between lectures, do not segregate themselves by religion. In the café up the road they sit in assorted groups of three and four sipping their mid-morning cokes. The young women are mostly easy to identify. Those who wear headscarves and long coats are Muslim; the ones with crosses round their necks, and wearing jeans, are clearly Christian. That is an incomplete guide. Numbers of the Muslim girls also wear jeans.

There are limits to camaraderie. The tabus are deep against close relationships across the religious divisions; not just between Muslims and Christians, but between the different Christian traditions. Nora, an Armenian Christian student, for instance, was adamant that she would never make close friends with an Orthodox or a Melchite (Greek Catholic) boy; let alone a Latin (Roman Catholic)! She was perfectly at ease with the two Muslim girls and a boy round the café table, and to them what she said seemed common sense.

Deep held as these religious beliefs may be, they do not lead to action. In Bethlehem University there is no indication of student religious activity. The Roman Catholic authorities are certainly careful not to seem dominant, and the politics that obsess the students bears no relation to their religion. So it was difficult to get a handful of students to say what their religious beliefs meant to them. They accepted their religion as they accepted the colour of their eyes. It was part of them, and they all certainly claimed to observe it, but it did not touch their minds. Once a student had established another's religious affiliation that was the end of the matter.

Yet from Bethlehem it is possible to learn something of the price of religious difference. Assa Dawoub is a qualified bookkeeper. Brought up as a Latin (Roman) Catholic, and married to one, he looked for a way of exercising his own strong Christian commitment. He became a Melchite (Greek Catholic), his wife converting with him, and he is now a deacon in that church. His long term hope, once he has qualified as an accountant, is to become a priest. His family have cut him off.

He also spoke of two nephews of his who, having been born in Bethlehem, went, while still young, with their parents to Kuwait. There they attended Muslim schools. When they returned to Bethlehem for a holiday, they refused to visit the Christian shrines. Instead they spat on them. All, however, their uncle explained, is now well. The boys are in a Christian school in Amman, and have come to profess the Christian religion.

To meet Palestinian Muslims and Christians, living alongside one another, united in their opposition to the Israeli military regime, helps to get into perspective the question of Christian–Muslim dialogue. In the west, it seems a matter of engaging in discussion before Islam gets too entrenched. Our host cultures have had a long tradition of absorbing immigrants. The scale of immigration over the past generation, and the obvious differences of race, make that now much more difficult. Yet as Christians in the west begin to reach out and engage responsive Muslims in dialogue, they are bracing themselves against the possibility of an unfamiliar religion treating the west as ripe for mission.

On the West Bank, the emphasis is on survival, identity and co-existence. There is no question of militant Islam, seeking to unite the smaller Christian population under the banner of the crescent. Religion has become too precious, too personal for that. So for Nora Bedrossian to change her allegiance would be to cut herself off from her roots. Around Jerusalem roots are very entangled, and go deep. Copt and Abyssinian Christians, tiny minorities both, claim seniority of tradition and cling on to their corners in the Church of the Holy Sepulchre. Greek Orthodox, far more numerous, have no interest in ecumenical dialogue, let alone interfaith explorations. They are not even prepared to have talks about talks about the date of Easter.

*　　*　　*

Then is interfaith dialogue only a nervous preoccupation of the liberal Christian west? The first International Conference of Interfaith Organisations took place in April 1985 at Ammerdown, near Bath. Apart from an Indian working at the World Council of Churches in Geneva, everyone was western European or North American and everyone was Christian. It was hard to enthuse about this gathering, despite the zeal of the organiser, reeking as it did of one more freeloading occasion. Indeed, to discover that the event had been subsidised by the Unification Church was enough to warrant a sense of disillusion. Could this collection of middle-aged executives of interreligious organisations really be the first wave of a new revelation?

The sessions set aside for interfaith worship were particularly disheartening. The chapel at Ammerdown is a simple one, lending itself to prayer. Those who had organised the conference were obviously anxious to avoid divisive words. So a group who were in fact all Christians met for a succession of worship periods whose chief feature was silence. Had it been inspired by Quaker openness, that silence might have freed us. Rather, it oppressed. We were tongue-tied because we were afraid to say anything. So we sat in rows, looking at the neck in front, wondering why we felt no sense of uplift.

There were things that we might have done together. Words are not the only means through which human beings express worship. Movement, light, music, incense, all are tried means. In their different ways, they feature in Jewish and Muslim as well as Christian worship. To have used them at Ammerdown might have helped us to hear what the one god might have to say to us. Instead we kept mum, only too conscious of our lop-sided origins. Tongue-tied Christians need others if there is to be interfaith dialogue. Otherwise we are like the Christian Embassy in Jerusalem, another cyst on the body politic.

TANTUR SEQUENCE

I

O holy 3 – in – 1
   Such is our D – I – Y
Thrice holy, holy, holy –
      Why?

Shallbewas the name
   Moses brought from on high;
O (ever ever ever)
      I

Abraham, Isaac, Jacob
   Tame triplicate the sky
Seed sacrifice and striving
      try

Father, Son, Spirit – three
   Starmen Christians descry
Claiming their unity
      Ply

All-merciful (all-wise,
   All powerful) – deny
The final prophet's claim,
      Die

Three peoples of the Book
   Rehearse your triple cry
Under the omniscient
      Eye.

2
Return to Jerusalem

"Ladies and gentlemen, on our right we have David's Tower. This is where the shepherd king wrote the Psalms. Note the height of the tower. King David received his inspiration through the east wind from the desert, which blew directly in through that window."

Of course it is fanciful nonsense. But, Canon John Wilkinson assured us, we should not be afraid of fancy. At this spot and in something of this manner a sixth century guide would have started to conduct his Christian pilgrims round the holy city. That old tower would be their first landmark as they entered Jerusalem by the Jaffa gate.

So the former Director of the British School of Archaeology in Jerusalem began leading his party on a tour of Byzantine Jerusalem. Some three hundred years after Constantine, and still officially known by its Latin name of Aelia Capitolinis, the city was the uncontested chief shrine of the Christian world. Islam had yet to emerge out of the deserts away to the south. The Jews had been scattered after the sack of Jerusalem in AD 70 and the final crushing of Bar Kochba's rebellion in AD 123. The few Jews left in the city were beneath notice.

Already Christian cracks were beginning to show. Abyssinian Christians, looking back to the ministry of St. Philip, had established their hold on the Church of the Holy Sepulchre, uneasy fellow custodians with their neighbours, the Egyptian Copts. To the Christian pilgrims from Europe both groups were suspect: monophysite heretics who refused to accept that Christ was fully human.

For most of Christendom, the Councils of the Church culminating in Chalcedon (AD 451) had polished the faith into a form still generally recognisable. That faith had spread far across the world. Missionaries had taken it to the furthest known island, Ireland, where it put down its own deep roots. It had spread along the North African seaboard, and far up the Nile.

Eastwards it had gone into Persia, and beyond into India, where Christians looked to doubting Thomas as the founder of their church. It was beginning to make its way into central Asia, along the silk routes towards China. Only on the edge of the known world had it yet to penetrate: to the Scythian wastes of Russia, and the pagan forests of Scandinavia. In due time it might reach there too. For had not Christ promised that faith in God through him was for all the world?

Jerusalem was the hub of that world, where Asia, Africa and Europe met. So the wide-eyed Byzantine pilgrim came and opened his eyes to its wonders. From the Jaffa gate he followed his guide to the church of the Holy Sepulchre. There he could gaze with awe at the rift in the rock below where the cross had stood, and then climb the stairway to reverence the site of Calvary. Only a few paces away (for St. John's gospel assured him that it was nigh) he could kiss the marble of the tomb from which his Saviour had been raised.

His tour did not end there. Through the warren of the suq his guide took him next to Pilate's house. There he could inspect the ruins of Roman splendour, and reflect on his faith that had outlasted the might of empire. From there the tour took him to the pool of Bethesda, an elaborate system of waterworks with its gleaming colonnade. He was then standing at the place where (St. John's gospel again) Christ had healed the paralytic who was never quick enough to get in when an angel troubled the waters.

To follow such a tour now calls for tunnel vision. In the fourteen or fifteen centuries since Byzantine pilgrims looked with awe upon the holy shrines of their faith, Jerusalem has become overlaid with encrustation upon encrustation of competitive piety. It is enough to leap the intervening centuries and consider simply the succession of monumental piles by which the empires of the 19th and 20th centuries have staked their claims.

There in the north-eastern corner of the old city flies the tricolour. St. Anne's Roman Catholic Cathedral was first offered by the Porte to Queen Victoria. She turned it down, and accepted Cyprus instead. So the cathedral, revered as the birthplace of the Virgin Mary, came into the hands of the Second Empire. Kaiser Frederick's Prussia was not to be outdone. The Lutheran Church of the Holy Redeemer, with the highest spire in the old city, is a monument to German imperialism. It is also a witness to an Anglo-German proposal that foundered. In 1840 the German Lutheran Church proposed sharing a bishopric in Jerusalem with the Church of England, turn and turn about. It sounded a practical scheme for establishing a mainline Protestant presence in Jerusalem. It never materialised. One effect it has was to push J. H. Newman and his followers one step nearer Rome. It was a naked example of states seeking to use their national churches for their own ends, and trampled over Anglican claims not to have forfeited (as the Lutherans had) their unbroken tradition as part of the western Catholic Church.

Within the old city itself the Church of England had in 1843 built Christchurch. Unlike the Germans they could find no site within the walls for a cathedral, so during the thirty years (1863–93) that Holy Redeemer was being built, a mile to the north the C of E countered with St. George's, a cantoonment owing more to Aldershot than Oxford. Over the same period Tsarist Russia established its presence. The onion domes of the Orthodox Church of Gethsemane parody their origins. Not to be excluded, down by the railway station the Church of Scotland built St. Andrew's kirk. The last of the powers to hoist their flag were the Americans. The Rockefeller Museum stands just outside the walls, on the north-east corner. Museum it may be, rather than a church, but its hexagonal tower is so much in the mould of early 20th century church architecture that it easily passes muster.

Between the Byzantine remains and the monuments of recent empires, Jerusalem has stratum upon stratum of other occupants. The great schism of AD 1058 gave the Eastern Orthodox church a headstart. Still theirs is the most powerful presence. A couple of centuries later came the Franciscans, named by Pope Gregory IX as guardians of the holy shrines. Up by the new gate the sign on their building shows how they maintain their presence: "Terra Sancta Strictly Private No Entry". In turn came the Greek Catholics (the Melchites), the Armenians, and the various competing orthodoxies of the middle east. All this is not the new Jerusalem of vision, but the old, of history.

In amongst the years of Christian presence are the Muslims.

According to Muslim belief, the Prophet made a miraculous night flight to this most distant of holy places, and the hoofprint of his horse is there on the sacred black rock for the faithful to venerate. The rock, also sacred to Jews as the place where Abraham sought to sacrifice Isaac, is canopied by the exquisite Dome of the Rock, built in 691 CE, an early witness to the rapid spread of Islam. Along with its neighbour the Al Aqsa Mosque, it rightly provides the most celebrated view of the old city. The spaciousness of their setting on the Temple mount contrasts with the clutter of the rest of the old city.

Within the walls of the old city, the only other open area is the place created by the Israeli administration around the western wall. Under that administration the old city is officially sacrosanct to three monotheistic faiths. The state of Israel has resisted all suggestions that it should be put under United Nations mandate. Instead the Israelis have for nearly twenty years now maintained their pledge that the faithful of all three traditions may without let or hindrance visit their holy shrines.

The Israelis claim priority for Jewish rule. Professor Zev Verblowski, of the Hebrew University, argues the case in a pamphlet made widely available for tourists, and goes round the world lecturing on the subject. His argument is simple. The Jews were here first, and it is their one shrine, the relic of the temple that is no more. Christians have a strong claim, but a subordinate one. The Muslim claim is much weaker: to them Jerusalem stands third to Mecca and Medina. Therefore Jerusalem should be in Jewish hands; and it is.

The municipality even employs an official to serve as secretary of the Jerusalem Interfaith Association. Jacob Emanuel is a podgy Israeli, about 40. With a damp handshake he greets his visitor. His office is a room in a private house in Rehavia. It is a cautious exploratory interview. Languidly he mentions a couple of very obvious names, but promises to find more later. A couple of days later he telephones to offer a further meeting. Has he meantime been checking one's credentials. For at this second meeting he is altogether brisker. He has a good dozen names to reel off, and they all sound very interesting. The growing frustration is whether there will be time to meet them all.

For already the occupational hazard of a television researcher obtrudes. People are away; or ring, and the phone will be answered in Hebrew. "Inglit . . . ?" (meaning, do you speak English?) breaks no ice. Sometimes German helps. Clearly the number of unmade contacts is far larger than the tally of successful ones. There is a lot of pot-luck in this business. To make a comprehensive study of interfaith activity in and around Jerusalem would call for months of enquiry; nobody should take a television series, however impressive, as definitive.

Along with those suggested by Mr Emanuel, preliminary homework suggests other leads to follow. One of them is the educational work of Alouph Hareven of the Van Leer Institute. The Dutch author and artist who delighted children of the 1930s with "Living things for Lively Youngsters" gave his name to this magnificent place of learning that fosters all sorts of sociological study. Mr Hareven's work lies in devising courses for Israeli and Arab teenagers. The principle behind it is that all future citizens of Israel should know something about each other.

It takes two visits to the Van Leer Institute to make contact. That is with Mrs Nurin, Mr Hareven's imperturbable secretary. For he is away, lecturing in the States. He will be back in a few weeks, and would no doubt be glad to take part in the programme. His diary is produced, and a tentative date for filming pencilled in. Subsequently it turns out to be a very worthwhile interview.

Then there are the fixers. Meeting Yvette Mimram at the time felt like a useful stroke of luck. An American Jew living in Jerusalem shared the taxi up from the airport, and showed interest in our plans. He gave us Yvette's name; she turned out to be running a travel agency. Being businesslike, her first interest was to secure ours, but then her enthusiasm took over, and she began speaking of the International Congress of Youth that she was arranging. It was linked to the World Congress for Religion and Peace, but it was to be even more positive. Gather a hundred or more young people in Jerusalem for a few days, and the city would show itself in its true colours, as the one place in the world from which peace would flow.

Ms Mimram comes from Morocco, a Sephardi. Most of the Israelis who dominate affairs originate from central Europe and are Ashkenazi Jews. Before they learned Hebrew, their *lingua franca* was German-based Yiddish. The Sephardim are mainly the Jews of the Mediterranean world, though in the 17th century they spread to the Netherlands and to England. Their common tongue is Ladino, derived from Spanish. In returning to Israel they have mostly made a less drastic change of climate and environment than the Jews from middle Europe. Along with the oriental Jews, gathered in from the Arab world, they seem more comfortably at home in this middle eastern setting.

Mrs Michael Krupp is Ashkenazi; she is French, and comes from Algeria. Her husband is a German Lutheran pastor who teaches at the Hebrew University. They have four children, whose first language is Hebrew. Ein Karem, an old village folded in a dale on the western outskirts of the city, is their home. It is a venerable building, originally the olive press of the nearby convent. To be with the Krupps is to savour to the full the sense of this precious ancient land calling its children home to make it good. Around their house their vegetables grow in profusion. Already the artichokes are nearly ripe for harvesting, and in the next plot the maize is well advanced. Around the walls of the house oranges hang in festoons, and on an old fig tree the fruit is beginning to form. Linger here, sipping fresh lemon and quoting the happy lines of the old prophets, and it would be almost possible to forget that there is tension in Israel, and that others aspire to these acres.

Michael Krupp is secretary of the Jerusalem Rainbow. In his late 40s he has lived in Israel for many years, and recently published a book on Zionism and the State of Israel. The book gives an historical sketch of Zionism over the past century, and then looks at the present. As a German, Krupp is particularly sensitive to the charge that Israel, in its handling of its Arab population, is being Fascist. In his eyes the present "grand coalition" government in which Shimon Perez and Yishtak Shamir rotate as Prime Minister and Deputy is a measure of the state's political stalemate. By its invasion of Lebanon it lost much sympathy in the western world (in particular the United States), and now has to learn to live, not as a western enclave in the Levant, but as a part of the middle east. He finds little comfort in the reiterated cries of peace, yet the initiative lies with Israel. The state cannot expect peace without making some concession towards the Palestinians.

Then what hope does he see in interfaith dialogue? Could that in its modest way contribute to the easing of the situation? He hesitates to say yes. Jerusalem Rainbow seems rather faded at present. Twenty years ago George Appleton, then Anglican archbishop in Jerusalem, had great hopes for it. He took no notice of the criticisms of those in his cathedral close who named him "Rabbi Appleton". In the mid-70s another colourful Anglican, Murray Rogers, formerly a CMS missionary in India, had set up his little "ashram" in the heart of the old city, and for a time it had seemed as if by importing something of the tolerance of Indian religion into the dialogue, he could help Christians and Jews and Muslims to be more open with one another. Too quickly, he earned the mistrust of all sides, and was expelled from the group. Now he is in Hong Kong.

And now, it seems, Jerusalem Rainbow hardly knows how to make its contribution to interfaith dialogue. There is a programme of meetings, but not many people come, and sometimes they are cancelled. Michael Krupp's eyes only lit up when he reverted to talking about his own family. There indeed was a miniature rainbow. Across the divides of language and religion, with his enchanting wife he speaks equally German and French. He happily accepts that she is Jewish, and that their children are Israeli, therefore to be brought up as Jewish. And practising? Essentially, came the answer, the Jewish religion is the religion of the home. The Friday evening seder was the high point of the family week. That, and the Hebrew language, and government schools, ensured the identify of the family. Yet he did not want his children to forget that he was Christian, and German. They had been to visit his family in Germany, and relations of his had stayed with them in Ein Karem. His own relations were most conscious of strain, but then, as he calmly reasoned, that is a tiny part of the price that Germans have to pay for what their government did to the Jews within his lifetime. He did not use the word "holocaust".

Yet he did agree, and gladly, to be filmed at Yad Vashem, the Israeli national memorial to that terrible memory. Within those sombre concrete walls the record of the horror is restrained. There is enough to make sure that nobody forgets, yet the eternal flame which is the centrepiece carries both an image of the belching chimneys and light to kindle hope.

In his book, Michael Krupp makes much of Martin Buber. Buber (1878–1965) is the Jewish philosopher *par excellence* of this century whom Christians have wanted to claim as a theologian. His concept of the I-Thou relationship between man and God filled Christian ministers in the 1930s and 1940s with excitement. Here was a Jewish thinker talking in language with which they could identify. He brought into focus the enquiries of psychology, and challenged the fashionable view that faith was all auto-suggestion.

To Krupp, Buber's importance is what he had to say about Israel. Writing before the foundation of the state, but when the tide of Zionism was running strong, Buber stressed the spiritual nature of Israel. It was to be the Kingdom of God, working through and beyond his peculiar people the Jews. But Buber was no simple advocate of a theocratic state. He was not pressing the claims of Orthodox Judaism against the secular tide. To do that would simply be to transfer the repressive practice of middle Europe to the Judaean hills. He had in mind something more open, a land when people would indeed acknowledge the claims of religion, but be ready to admit their variations in practice and look the world in the eye.

* * *

Side by side, the red granite figures, larger than life, peer ahead of them. One has a flowing turban, immediately identifiable as Mohammed. The other two are bearded figures, in the prime of life, similar in appearance and both noble. "You must make your own choice," says Jacov Kalman, seeing his visitor's puzzlement. "One is Moses, yes; one is Jesus. You are free to decide which is which."

For this is the spacious lobby of the Martin Buber Institute, of which Dr Kalman is director. The institute is housed in the lower ground floor of a building that forms part of the Mount Scopus campus of the Hebrew University. A high strip of tinted window at ground level throws an aqueous light into space. It is an irregular rectangle, with narrow concrete columns supporting the floor above, and so designed that the sculpture occupies attention.

Christians make free with images. It takes a moment to recall the deep tabu, both in Judaism and Islam, against graven images. Yet one of these is Mohammed, one of these is Moses, and Jesus along them. Here they all are, with that tease of uncertainty about the two with beards. The immediate thought is that this sculpture would make perfect caption title for the television series: "One God . . . Three Gods?" It will not do. These are men. There is no nimbus, no distortion to make them into ikons. Whatever they are, whoever they are, they are not pretending to be gods; not God, anyway.

Dr Kalman understands the dilemma, and suggests another possibility. He leads the way into a room that reproduces Buber's study. It is full of heavy German furniture, and with an oil lamp on the desk. Perhaps we might be glad to film in here. For if we are looking for those who have been touched by more than one of the three religions, or who have touched more than one, then Buber must be high on our list. It is an enticing possibility. The only trouble is that Buber is dead. Television speaks more easily through people who are alive.

From that moment it was a matter of politeness to let Dr Kalman explain his work. He tells of his co-operation with Sister Teresa of the Mount Sion convent to create a religious education curriculum for older school pupils that can be used in all Israeli government schools. A visitor from England where educationalists fret to make undemanding sense of the 1944 Education Act's requirements for religious education could not but be impressed. For here was a secular state taking religion seriously. In the eyes of the band of secularist militants, Israel has already made more than enough concessions to religion. It is impossible to have a civil wedding in Israel. All marriages must be conducted by the accredited ministers of one religion or another. Bit by bit religion claws its way back into everyday life.

In England the drift is the other way. Under the guise of encouraging comparative religion, so as to understand our next door neighbours, educationalists draw the teeth of religion. They want it studied through the wrong end of the telescope. The trend is not as new as some Christians fear. Sixty years ago G. K. Chesterton was already attacking the problem:

"I do seriously recommend the imaginative effort of conceiving the Twelve Apostles as Chinamen. In other words, I recommend these critics to try and do as much justice to Christian saints as if they were pagan sages." (The Everlasting Man, London, 1925)

For Jacov Kalman and Sister Teresa do not see their work as comparative religion, which treats all the ingredients of its study as curious phenomena. Rather their intention is to devise a curriculum that will enable students to examine their own religion in the light of the other two. Their basic premise is that to live well people have to go on living within the religion into which they have been born, but instead of treating the other religions as curios, they should seek to understand how they too seek to treat the range of human need. In that way they may come to treat their own religion with the seriousness that it invites.

"Then it is a question of truth, and how it is given to us." Dr Kalman may owe his post to the sociology of religion. He spoke from the side of the angels.

Up the stairs from the aquarium of the Martin Buber Institute, daylight glares. The creamy Jerusalem stone intensifies the sunlight. Dominating this courtyard at the high point of the campus stands the Harry S. Truman Institute. Even before 1967 Mount Scopus was a Jewish enclave in Jordanian-held territory, and through the Mandelbaum Gate they came to establish their lovely set of buildings on the highest of the hills overlooking the city of Jerusalem.

Anyone who earlier the same morning had been in the crowded playground of Bethlehem University could only make stark comparisons. There must be much the same comparison between the black and white universities of South Africa. In Bethlehem the plaster peels from the disregarded statues of the saints. Muslims and Christian students flock to chatter oblivious of Sacred Heart and Little Flower. Here on Mount Scopus everything gleams, and discreet plaques record the millions of dollars that have gone into creating this place of learning. The official figures say that eleven per cent of the student body at the Hebrew University is Palestinian; no apartheid here. Two gum-chewing American young women are the only ones in evidence. Like the faces of past presidents on Mount Rushmoor, the three interrelated figures in the Martin Buber Institute stare side by side into space. They do not look at each other.

II

Jerusalem: from shrine to shrine
   We track an archaeologist
   Who scorns the present to insist
Our pilgrimage be Byzantine,

And does it well: "Here's David's tower
   Here, wind-inspired, he made the Psalms . . ."
   "Alms, for the love of Allah, alms . . ."
"Scram! Don't disturb our holy hour."

So at the foot of Golgotha
   (The queue's too long for Calvary's stair)
   We hail the cleft rock and repair
To ('nigh at hand') the Sepulchre

And kiss the stone: not piety,
   We're reassured, but "Welcome, place;"
   In kissing you we catch your grace
With sanctified sobriety.

And here was Pilate's residence
   (An Arab brat comes snuffling past
   And interrupts John's gospel's vast
Sketchbook of glory and pretence).

Gethsemane; a monk hids shush;
   We, sotto voce, say our lines
   Remembering eager Byzantines
Who used to stink and shove and push.

The Mount of Olives and Ascension,
   And suddenly a routed mosque
   Lends credence to the bal de masque . . .
They've gone. I'm left. God's intervention?

3
Tantur

The Tantur Ecumenical Institute for Advanced Theological Research is another foundation dating from the time of Pope Paul VI. It was established in 1968, as a centre for study and dialogue. It provided an obvious base for an enquiry such as ours.

The institute is easy to find. It stands on the right of the road between Jerusalem and Bethlehem. Some four miles from the centre of the city, it lies just with boundaries of annexed Jerusalem. A little further down the road running into Bethlehem is the line marking the beginning of occupied Judaea, but there is no evidence of it. Up on the hill westwards of Tantur the hard cream stone of the suburb of Gilo catches the morning sun. It was the first of the circle of suburbs to be built after the 1967 war, and like a parody of Bath the crescents of apartment blocks swoop their way over the hillside.

Tantur has room to itself. Six-foot walls surround its hundred acres, and the approach to the buildings is up a drive through an olive grove. A bend in the road, and there squats an ancient gatehouse. A stone shield above the archway is emblazoned with a spindly Maltese cross, heralding the property of the Knights of St. John. In front of the gatehouse a standard roadsign bars access, with an arrow directing visitors to the right. The lane leads round to the back of the complex of modern buildings and gives some appreciation of their scale.

There are two main blocks, linked by a portico. The building to the fore, two lofty storeys high, is in the form of a hollow square. It is the library block, and consists mainly of a spacious reading area, air-conditioned and inviting scholarship. Stands in the centre display the enormous range of journals that the library receives. A quick glance shows most of them to be in English, mainly American publications, along with others in German, French, Italian, and other European languages. There are a few publications in Arabic, and even one or two in Hebrew. Ecumenical research is clearly a major discipline.

In the basement and on the floor above there are books and books and books, and various offices and study rooms lead off the main library area. The southern side of the square houses a large conference room, complete with all the trappings of modern learning.

A noticeboard gives some indication of the range of enquiry. There is the office of the Rector, of the Director of Christianity in the Holy Land, of the Director of Peace Studies, of the Director of Finance and Administration.

The library block lies to the north of the great quadrangle that is the central feature of Tantur. It is laid out in formal flowerbeds, with wide paved walks between. Already, in March, the beds were bright with the flowers of spring: petunias, marigolds, irises and a host of Mediterranean flora gave a bright display under the uncertain sky. A few old olive trees remained, and a couple of eucalyptus to give the sub-tropical touch.

The centre of this great space strikes curiously bare, consisting of a large circle of flagstones. With only the gatehouse and a retaining wall on its eastern side, to the west and south the quadrangle is enclosed by the other main building of Tantur. This is a three-storey block, running straight along the western length, but to the south shaped like three sides of an octagon. It contains mostly living quarters, a corridor running right through, with rooms to either side.

In all this something seemed to be missing. That was it, there was no sign of a chapel. A glance at the architect's model, on display in the reception area, provided the explanation. On the model the chapel stands in the centre of the quadrangle, a fanciful winged building looking like a miniature Sydney Opera House, quite in contrast to the plain lines of the rest. It has not been built.

What for the duration serves as the worship room is a downstairs cube at the south-eastern extremity of the range. It is concrete and cavernous. In the centre stands a slab laid on a chunk of rock. Facing in towards it on each of the four sides is a row of low-backed black leather upright chairs. By contrast with this austere modernity, one corner of the cube houses a vintage harmonium, no doubt passed on by some well-wisher as a temporary measure.

It would indeed be easy to wander round Tantur in the middle of the morning and see nobody. But, no. "I'm Father O'Connor, call me Jim", and a friendly American Jesuit extends a hand of welcome. He has due right to act as host. For in establishing the Institute in 1968, Paul VI put its administration in the care of the Jesuits of Notre Dame University, Indiana. Still it is in their charge, and it did not take long to hear of Fr Hessburg, SJ, who from that distance holds the strings.

It is another Indianan that Jim O'Connor takes me to meet. Landrum Bolling is taking his mid-morning tea. He is the former president of Earlham College, Richmond, Indiana, a foundation of the Society of Friends. Having previously served as its President, he is for the time being acting as Rector of Tantur. Blue eyes of Scandinavian origin look out keenly from beneath his shaggy brows. With his cragged face, he must be somewhere into his seventies. There is firmness there, altogether a noble head, and a man that commands respect. Somewhat portly, even when he appears in open necked shirt and shorts, he still has an unmistakable presence.

The letter posted from London a fortnight previously, explaining the mission and asking for accommodation, has not yet arrived. The whole matter needs explaining from scratch but Bolling readily offers a room and whatever help he and his colleagues can give. Inevitably the mention of mutual friends seals the arrangement. Tantur has its British Committee, of which Bishop Robin Woods is chairman, and the then Dean of Canterbury, Victor de Waal, an active member.

Indeed only the previous week they have both been there. There has been a gathering to mark the departure after four years of the previous Rector, an Englishman, Donald Nicholls. Bolling is acting as Rector until a more permanent arrangement can be made.

He has inherited what immediately seems to be a lively going concern. Tantur functions on the model of an academic institute, and arranges a yearly programme, divided into semesters or terms (both expressions are in use, and reflect the Anglo-American character of the Institute). Primarily it sees itself as a place designed to attract scholars, who are invited for three or six months to come and use its library facilities, and its contacts in Jerusalem, and so pursue their particular interest in the general field of ecumenical studies. At any one time there are about half a dozen of them in residence, their numbers limited largely by lack of scholarship funds to support their visits.

Then there are the Maryknolls. The Maryknoll Fathers are an American Roman Catholic society of missionary priests, working all over the third world. They have arranged to use Tantur as a study centre, and about twenty priests at a time gather there for a six month programme of study which the society itself arranges.

The senior staff itself is small, and in 1985 was in the process of change. Clearly Bill Klassen, the Director of Peace Studies, is the effective deputy. He is a Mennonite minister, American by birth, but coming to Tantur after a long spell in Simon Fraser University, British Columbia, where he had served as an administrator. Little known in Britain, the Mennonites are an old established Protestant church with a strong tradition of pacifism. It is not unfair to say that they are like the Quakers only with a traditional form of church government, including an ordained ministry.

Since he came to Tantur with his wife Donna in 1982, Klassen has built up his division to the point where it is now the most significant aspect of Tantur's activities. For an Ecumenical Institute, Peace Studies at first seem a by-way. The argument advanced for its prominence in the Institute's activities is quite simple. Not to have them would be to ignore the realities of Israel. It might in principle be desirable for the Institute to concentrate solely on ecumenical studies, but a location on the border of annexed Jerusalem and the West Bank cries out for the Institute's attention.

On the Institute's notice board there was a recent press-cutting from the English-language weekly edition of the Jerusalem Arabic daily *Al Kuds*. It describe the lone fight of an aged Palestinian Arab to hang on to his piece of ground. There was reference in the article to the part that the Institute had played in helping his fight.

"For, look, he is only just up the road." From the windows of the common-room, quarter of a mile away up the hill under the walls of Gilo a green ridge-tent is clearly visible. On close inspection it proves to be surrounded by a pile of household effects. Then the story comes out. This Palestinian widower, in his eighties, has for forty years and more been tenant of a smallholding on this site. He has paid his rent punctually, and been altogether a model tenant. Some years ago his landlord sold the property to a Jew in Los Angeles, but for the time being the tenancy was undisturbed. Then, not so long ago, came notice to quit. The old man took no notice and went on cultivating his patch and paying his rent. Without warning, one night in August 1983, two armed men arrived at his door and ordered him out. They chucked out his belongings and bulldozed his house. He was left stranded. The Red Cross provided him with the tent, pitched within a few yards of the ruins of his home, and his two sons are fighting his case. Dorothy Nicholls, wife of the then Director, took up the cudgels and wrote to Mr Kollek. In due course she received a courteous reply, and at least the case is promised careful investigation. Such activity has a price to pay. Naomi Teasdale, the English speaking personal assistant to the redoubtable Mayor of Jerusalem, Teddy Kolleck, learned that her visitor was staying at Tantur. She stiffened. "Tantur", she said, "is getting into peace. Peace is dangerous."

Tantur could not stand by and ignore that scene on its doorstep. At night, from the roof of the Institute, it is possible to see further. Two Arabs, Costas and Abdul, are the nightwatchmen at Tantur, and invite friendship. One night they lead the way on to the extensive flat roof of the library building. But for the difficulties of photographing in the dark, the panorama lends itself to the film. To the north, Jerusalem sprawls across its undulations. The flares of orange neon lighting rise in waves. At their crest, to the left, is the unmistakable tower of the Jerusalem Hilton, standing sentinel at the city's western gate.

To our west, only half a mile away, are the glaring street lights of Gilo, and the lights in the apartment blocks being switched off now that it is towards midnight. Between Gilo and the city itself are pools of darkness, and more of them as our eyes retrace the contours back towards Mount Scopus over to the north east.

"Palestinian villages," Costas explains; "Curfew." The matter needs no further explanation. Then the two nightwatchmen lead the way to the southern side of the roof, and we are looking towards Bethlehem. Constellations of small white street lamps mark its pattern of roads. Otherwise there is very little light, except that in the centre glows a six-pointed star. It is not the two inverted triangles that form the Star of David. There is only the outline. It is the star of Bethlehem, illuminating Manger Square.

The Institute's day begins early. The godly are invited to use the meditation room from six-thirty onwards. It is adjacent to the worship room, a smaller cube, with a few kneeling stools in it and not much else. The windows are shut, and it is airless, and one visit more than satisfies inquisitive piety. Then comes breakfast at 7.30, and fifty wideawake residents serve themselves, ready to indulge in bright conversation at the round tables which seat eight. Breakfast, like other meals, owes its catering to the officer's mess. There are grapefruit and hard-boiled eggs to be had at this hour, or on some days trayfuls of scrambled egg in wodges. The coffee invites its daily ration of mild grumbling. The tea stews, to discourage latecomers.

Lunch is the main meal of the day, almost always with meat, sliced and roasted in the western manner, rather than chunky and skewered. The vegetables and the desserts belong to this traditional good plain cooking. For supper there is kedgeree, or curry, again produced to an expatriate formula. Citrus fruit is in season, but the best Jaffas have gone for export, and these must be last autumn's apples. It is too early in the year for figs. There is always goat's cheese.

Lunch, when the non-resident staff are present, provides an easy opportunity to get to know something of Tantur. The rector's secretary, Barbara Gibson, is a friendly young woman from Scotland. She has been working in Tantur three years, and is in no hurry to leave. Sitting next to her is another young woman, Jane Selby. Despite her name, she is Arab, from Bethlehem, a graduate of the university, and thankful to find an interesting job on the doorstep. George is another graduate of Bethlehem. He takes his turn on the reception desk. It does not seem much of a job for a graduate, but he too is thankful to have it. There are so few opportunities. He says that he is studying in his spare time for a higher degree, and he is certainly clever and academically minded. But he does not talk with much conviction about his higher studies. He sees no future for himself as an Arab in the Israeli occupied West Bank, and like many of his contemporaries thinks eagerly of emigrating to the west. Like everyone else seems to do, he has a cousin in New York. But he is very ready to consider Britain, and enquires with such tempting eagerness about the prospects of further study and employment in London that it seems churlish to make too much of the British government's fresh wave of discouragement to overseas students, or of the difficulties that British graduates have in finding themselves satisfactory jobs. For George, meanwhile, Tantur provides an interesting steady job. He looks after the residents and visitors with warmth and constant helpfulness, but as a locally recruited younger member of staff, clearly does not expect to have any involvement in its affairs. Nor, for all that he is an Arab Christian whose faith means something important to him, is he encouraged to participate in the Institute's proceedings.

As the politics of Tantur unravel over the following days, something of the fragility of the Institute begins to emerge. When it began in the late 1960s, four Benedictine monks came to live there, to form an inner community of worship.

It was set up with good intentions, and plenty of money was forthcoming for the buildings, even though it stopped short of building the chapel. But then it is not altogether clear, certainly not now with the monks gone these past five years, what purpose a swaggering chapel might serve. Among its senior posts Tantur has no Director of Worship, though Bolling speaks of creating one. Without such co-ordination there is a hole in the middle of all that the Institute sets out to do and be.

This hole became quickly apparent in the course of the visit. At any one time Tantur has between forty and fifty visitors in residence, though it can accommodate at least twice that number. They are mostly American or British, coming from a variety of Christian traditions. The prevailing arrangement is that at six o'clock each evening there should be a service of up to half an hour in the worship room, each week conducted according to a particular tradition sufficiently represented amongst those in residence.

It so happened that in the first few days of my visit it was the turn of the Anglicans. To join in Evening prayer, with a hymn and the canticles sung, was a reassuringly familiar activity. The following week it was the turn of the Lutherans, of whom there was quite a United States contingent. So we were treated to a homily every evening, moralistic in tone, and sang two or three sentimental hymns to tunes in minor keys that gave the lady at the harmonium scope to show her prowess.

To be so easily irritated by that experience, which should not have felt so totally foreign, was a sharp reminder of the pain of ecumenism. Talk and brave notions cost little. Undergoing worship in an alien mode, and trying to join in and belong, costs much more. It was humbling to see how fully the Roman Catholic priests in residence took part in these services. All their instinct and devotion must have been very much further away from it.

But then they were having their daily mass. There was something hole-in-corner about it. Rather like El Al flights, which vary from their published schedule to evade terrorists, so these masses took place with no public notice, at a different time each day. Others were really not encouraged to attend. For that after all would raise the awkward question of intercommunion, at which Tantur is not alone in jibbing.

On Sundays there is more decorum. An Anglican eucharist or a Protestant form of worship alternate, with the expectation that those in residence will attend and take full part. It is, however, perfectly accepted that individuals may prefer to attend worship in a church of their own tradition somewhere else in the neighbourhood. There is no shortage of churches.

Uncertainty about how to worship as a community seems the key to Tantur's problem of identity. Clearly it began as a confident gesture of Roman Catholic missionary endeavour, in the best sense of that phrase. For the Institute was not in any sense out to proselytise. Its intention was straightforward and admirable, to provide, on the edge of Jerusalem, a place of godliness and learning. If the word "ecumenical" in its title emphasised dialogue between Christians of different traditions, that was proper enough, but from the first the intention was to be open to dialogue with Jews and Muslims as well.

Thus now, at least, the Institute as a matter of policy seeks to have on its staff at least one or two members of other faiths. The assistant librarian is Chaim Levi, a secular Jew who lives in Tel Aviv. Professionally qualified, he finds his work challenging and interesting, and has no qualms about being employed by a

Christian institution. Nor do his friends find anything odd about it. Much more critical is his brother, who has, as he puts it, 'turned religious' and as an Orthodox Jew will not now entertain his own brother at his table, whatever his employment.

Amongst the academic staff there are no Muslims, but quite a number amongst the supporting staff. Even so, the majority of them are Christians, since they mostly come from Bethlehem, only a mile down the road, and Bethlehem for reasons not altogether surprising is a Christian town.

Despite its strong Christian character, Tantur has over the years managed to present itself as a centre for encouraging dialogue at least with Jews. Its records also mention occasions when learned Muslims have come to give conferences, but under Israeli administration most of the Muslims who might be interested in learned interfaith dialogue have gone elsewhere. That is why, in making the television series "One God . . . Three Gods?" we recognised the need additionally to film in Cairo.

Interfaith dialogue is heady. Tantur is not the only institution in Jerusalem that has found it difficult to develop and sustain. In its role as a Christian ecumenical centre it has plenty of main business to pursue. Here Dr Geraes Khouri holds the key. He is a Melchite (Greek Catholic) layman, who rejoices in the title of Director of Christianity in the Holy Land. Palestinian by origin, the European language in which this guarded academic of around 40 most comfortably works is Italian, and in that language his treatise on his subject is to be published.

As a Melchite, brought up in Galilee, he is well placed to understand the labyrinthine complexities of Christianity in the Holy Land. The Greek Catholic church, which in the Lebanon calls itself Maronite, is the heir of nine hundred years of schism between Rome and Constantinople. In the Holy Land now it is a growing communion. Unlike the Latin (Roman Catholic) church, which still has the smell of crusading imperialism about it, it is indigenous; but since it is a Uniate church, in communion with Rome, it is not cut off from dialogue with western Christianity.

The Greek Orthodox church is cut off, and content to be. It regards Rome as its supplanting rival. Alongside the secular politics of Israel, the politics of Christianity run on and on. In 1974 the Archimandrite of the Greek Patriarchate, a Chicago born double of the notorious Archbishop Marcincus, was complaining of the departure from Jerusalem of the Anglican Archbishop, George Appleton, and his replacement by a couple of Arabs. "We Orthodox," declared the archimandrite indignantly, "we need you Brits. You stand with us against these damned Latins."

A decade and more later, that attitude persists in frustrating any approaches from Tantur to the Greek Orthodox. For in their eyes Tantur is Latin. They would have no interest in coming to examine it in detail, or think anything of the presence of Quakers, such as Bolling, or Mennonites, such as Klassen, or even of the preponderance of Anglicans and mainstream American Protestants. To them, Tantur is somewhere the other side of the hill. Indeed, only a quarter of a mile from Tantur, on a facing knoll in the direction of Jerusalem, stands the Greek Orthodox monastery of St. Elias. Every one of Tantur's attempts to make contact with it, these past twenty years, evidently, have been unconditionally rebuffed. The Greek Orthodox do not want to know.

Around Christmas, there comes the round of diplomatic invitations. At that season even the Greek Orthodox Patriarchate is prepared to open its doors to the gallimaufry of schismatics, and offer them retsina and a restrained welcome. Much more hospitable to the collegiates of Tantur are the aboriginal Christians, the Abyssinians and the Copts. They love to welcome anybody who will bother to accept their invitation. So year by year a little party sets out from Tantur, goes to the home of the Coptic archbishop, to find him, rather like Miss Faversham in "Great Expectations" in festal array waiting for visitors who never come.

Greek Orthodox intransigeance is more than a matter of the dusty disputes of past ages. Politically, it is the church of the left. An Arab Christian citizen of Israel who belongs to the Greek Orthodox church is likely to vote DFPE, that is Communist, which has four members in the present Knesset. International politics come into it, too. The Soviet Union is consistently hostile to the state of Israel, despite her recent diplomatic moves, and it is widely accepted that Russian money supports the Greek Orthodox church. There is irony in the thought that a hundred and more years after Tsar Nicholas I made his country's mark at Gethsemane, his atheist successors should be continuing to support the cause.

So Tantur, with its American, Roman Catholic, backing can hardly expect to find it easy to engage in dialogue with the Greek Orthodox Patriarchate. Clearly those who run Tantur chafe at the strings that tie them to Notre Dame. Out of the gathering that marked Donald Nicholls' retirement one suggestion has begun to emerge that could give Tantur more room for manoeuvre. That is to put the Institute in the charge of a body chaired by the Archbishop of Canterbury. The argument is that Rome is too much to one side. Canterbury, as in the past, might provide the flag under which the Institute could progress.

For already the Institute enjoys a range of Christian support. Matching the Anglican character of the British committee, there is on the board of trustees the American born philanthropist John M. Templeton. For all his keen support for things English, and his pride in his British citizenship, he is a Presbyterian. Whether his well-endowed foundation might be prepared to give Tantur substantial backing only he and his closest advisers can decide. Certainly what the Institute needs if it is to have a fresh lease of life is wider active support than till now it has enjoyed.

In particular it could benefit from a strong local committee. Although the Institute is well known amongst the ecumenically minded of Jerusalem, they have never been encouraged to become closely involved in its affairs. Its programme of weekly lectures and seminars that runs from September till June has over the course of the years attracted from the city almost all the leading names in religious thinking, Jewish as well as Christian. Under successive administrations, these weekly events have varied from co-ordinated courses to successions of single events, with no common theme running through them. Now it is hard to escape the feeling that after nearly twenty years, Tantur has for the moment broken its finger nails on the rocks of Jerusalem. On those rocks lie many wrecks of hope. Generation after generation has sought to strike from them a trickle of water of hope, and the city is strewn with moribund institutions that have failed to fulfil their original intention. It would be sad, but not surprising, if Tantur were to be added to their number.

III

The wind sprawls where it lists,
   Baggaging the muezzin's call
   In contapuntal bawl
Against our eucharists.

Set in our solemn square
   Avoiding every eye
   We let that sound sail by,
Continuing in prayer.

One week as Anglicans
   We say Magnificat;
   Next week get God off pat
As hymnal Lutherans.

And sand-grained Roman priests
   Rise secretly at dawn
   To keep their Lord in pawn
And hug his feast of feasts.

Attractive Arab youth
   Look after all our needs;
   And who, I wonder, heeds
Their distance form our truth?

Yes, Jesus took a towel
   And bid us do the same;
   Oh, we are not to blame
Who've thrown off cope and cowl.

God is our Democrat
   (Maybe Republican)
   Brit or American
We've got him; that is that.

Tell, howling hurricane,
   Over West Bank (Judaea)
   If us you cannot hear
You're not American.

4
Father of Nations

For anyone planning to make television in Israel, the first port of call is at the office of the Ministry of the Press in Beit Agron, a modern block overlooking Independence Park in the heart of Jerusalem. The names of Sheila has been suggested as a first point of English language contact, and it is a matter of making an appointment and then marching briskly in past the uninterested armed guard. Sheila has heard it all many times before, and has her response pat. Except for military installations, there is no problem about filming anywhere in Israel. She listens a bit more to our proposals. "Perhaps you had better see Major Horowicz," she says, and leads the way to another office.

Major Horowicz, swarthy, trimly moustached, is the model military press officer. "Have a seat, call me Alex," he says. The delicate question is what about filming on the West Bank. "You mustn't call it that. It is Judaea and Samaria. 'West Bank', – why that could mean anywhere between the Jordan and the Mediterranean." After that firm rebuke, he softens. There should be no problem. If we have any difficulties, we should simply ask him, and he would be happy to furnish the necessary permits. "There is occasionally a little spot of bother," he explains, "and then we discourage foreign film crews."

With that much promise of *laisser-passer* secured, it is a matter of investigating the site that we have agreed should furnish our starting point, the tomb of Abraham in Hebron. Hebron is some thirty miles south of Jerusalem, and over the years has seen some of the most violent incidents between Arabs and Jews. It is an Arab city, but one where the most ardent Jewish believers in Israel's right to the whole land, the Gush Enenim, have been establishing their illegal settlements. In 1983 the Mayor of Hebron was seriously wounded when a bomb exploded under his car. Hebron university is constantly under surveillance as a breeding ground for Arab revolt.

This tatty Arab city houses the one shrine that is sacred to Jews, Christians and Muslims. Abraham is the father of all three religions, and this is where he is buried. The word "tomb" much underestimates the complexity of buildings that greet the visitor. It is the scale and has the outward appearance of a fortress, and a narrow lane leads round below high walls to the one point of entry. There a section of Israeli soldiers guard the entrance, which leads to a long flight of shallow steps. My companion on this visit was a lady in a wheelchair, and the steps looked daunting. One of the Israeli soldiers gladly helped me turn it into a sedan, but he was encumbered with his uzi rifle, and she had to hold it for him. The possibilities of using a wheelchair as a James Bond variation of the Trojan Horse provided us with plenty of laughs afterwards.

The top of the flight of steps leads into a succession of arched chambers and colonnades. The guide books label this as Mameluke architecture, dating from the Turkish conquest of the 13th Century. The first hall through which we passed certainly had the feeling of the mosque. Its floor was covered with Turkey carpets, and there were three or four white clad Muslims, with their distinctive white lace skull caps, busy at their devotions. We left them and moved into a sunlit patio, with a fountain playing in the middle, and wisteria gracing its walls. It is a peaceful place. Off one side of it leads the way into the heart of the shrine. It houses three large plaster clad cases, domed like old cabin trunks. An English speaking Jewish guide was explaining them to a small group. These are the tombs of Abraham, of Isaac and of Jacob. For whatever reason, Isaac's is rather larger than the other two. The three tombs stand well apart from one another. In this pillared space there is nothing else to see. It feels more like an antiquity than a place of devotion.

Our next concern was to see whether there was a supply of electricity, to which it would be possible to connect television lights. One of the curators discussed the question with interest, and led us proudly to the main source of power, which had every sign of having been installed by Allenby's conquering army in 1916. The curator assured us that it was in good working condition, and careful pacing measured how much length of cable we should need. It meant kneeling down to see where best to lay it.

So preoccupied, I almost bumped into somebody. It was a black cassock, and a staff. The bearded figure under the stovepipe hat looked gravely at this interruption to his progress. It was an Orthodox priest, leading a party of young seminarians, with their sprouting beards and sugarloaf hats of apprenticeship. The progress swept past. They were muttering some sort of prayer, telling beads perhaps.

In Israel everything is different, and nothing is to be taken as extraordinary. It took us a while to appreciate that in the Tomb of Abraham, as nowhere else, we had indeed seen Muslims, Christians and Jews sharing one holy place. The Muslims prostrated, the Jews learning, the Christians in procession. There was room enough for them all comfortably to ignore one another. Something of the same spirit must have brought them to the place. The last thing, quite clearly, that would have occurred to any of them would have been to engage with one another. Even at the tomb of their common father, Abraham's children keep themselves to themselves. Generations of inherited practice have grooved them into their own patterns of devotion. There is only one god, and the other two are pretenders.

Now it was a matter of securing permission to film. Clearly as the incident with the uzi gun had showed, military precautions at the Tomb of Abraham were not severe, and certainly "Alex" – Major Horowicz – had encouraged the idea that any permit should be obtained locally. Carrying the wheelchair back down the flight of steps, I raised the question with my amiable fellow-porter, Aaron. We should have to ask his officer, and so the captain was respectfully summoned. This young officer affected only to speak Hebrew, and so Aaron acted as interpreter. No doubt Aaron did his interpreting faithfully but what had seemed a simple question of asking permission to film in the tomb became one of diplomatic protocol. A middle-aged Englishwoman in a wheelchair and her escort, at this site, hardly looked like the forerunners of a TV crew out to film military secrets. Sheltering behind his language and his rank, the young captain clearly indicated that he carried the security of state upon his shoulders. In the end Aaron explained, apologetically, that it would mean going back to the headquarters at Beit Agron for a permit.

That was not the end of it. "Alex" was away for the day when I telephoned for an appointment. Try Friday morning (on the eve of *Shabbat* all government offices shut at noon). On Friday morning he was still not there. Sheila's advice was to go to the headquarters of the military administration in Ramallah, and she wrote down the name of the woman captain Rebecca who would sort it all out for me there. She was vague about the precise location of this military establishment. No Israeli who can help it ventures into Judaea or Samaria.

With the sands of Friday morning running out, a researcher bent on providing this crucial permit to film set out on the road to Ramallah. Barbed wire and an Israeli flag are the obvious signs of any military compound. At the first such place, somewhere on the northern fringes of annexed Jerusalem, the sentry on duty studies Sheila's English directions with no understanding. None of his companions in arms are any the wiser. They point northwards. So into the city of Ramallah, like Hebron, an Arab town, like Hebron, with its injured Mayor, like Hebron, with its university (Birzeit) constantly under review. It was no place for an Englishman to ask a passer-by where to find the headquarters of the Israeli military administration. But there, quite close to the university, with a tall radio-mast as its beacon, was the familiar compound with barbed wire and the Israeli flag. Another Israeli soldier studies without comprehension Sheila's precious scrap of paper. He motions his petitioner to take a seat on a rough bench under a makeshift awning. Two or three patient Arabs, waiting there with no doubt equally hopeless petitions, shove up to make room for this stranger.

Minutes tick by, and then the corporal comes. He has the barest English: "right, right, and then left" is the gist of it. Off again; but despite the even higher communications beacon that appears to be the goal of this quest, there is only barbed wire and no entry. Were the "rights" miscounted? Now the road seems to be leading back into Ramallah, and there – ah, that might help, is the police station. Again it is a matter of patient waiting, while the matter goes up the ranks, this time as high as the sergeant. This time the message is understood, and the directions are clear. The headquarters of the Israeli administration in Judaea and Samaria are a mile up the road, on the right.

That calls for driving past a sign with an unambiguous warning to motorists. Like the inscription above the cross, it uses three languages to ward the motorist of what is to come. "You are now entering Samaria. The administration takes no responsibility for your safety." But then just beyond the dip in the road is the familiar Israeli flag and barbed wire, and a high wall as well.

These battlements invite parking at a humble distance, and making the approach on foot. In any case the entrance is protected by a very unattractive device. There are spikes across the roadway, which only sink into their kennel when a guard inside presses the button which lifts the protecting barrier. A pedestrian can slip round the edge.

Again there is the altercation, quite familiar by this time, with the sentry on duty and his comrades. They in turn study Sheila's crumpled scrap of paper. Laconically – and, yes, there is something Spartan about Israel – they point where to go. It is not in here at all. It is down there; and down there is a building looking like a corporation toilet. Meekly the baffled investigator makes for it. There is nothing there. Back to the entrance again, and again the guards insist that down there is the way to go, down and round to the left. Down round the outside of the cantoonment, and left leads into a ploughed field. Well, perhaps they were right; but plodding through mud leads only to more mud, and no sign of any back door. This is ridiculous, and unworthy of one carrying a passport in the name of Her Britannic Majesty.

On the third return to the jagged entry, British grit is uppermost, till the commander of the guard telephones his chief. Unexpectedly, the answer is come in, and a suspicious escort leads the way to the office of Captain Rebecca. Even then, she is not in her office, and has to be winkled out of the one next door where she has been having a chat.

She makes up for it all. She is delightful, charm itself in the accents of Brooklyn. Captain Rebecca accepts an English cigarette and carefully considers the request for a permit to film in the Tomb of Abraham. "But that is in Hebron," she says, "and Hebron is in Judaea. This is the military administration for Samaria. Judaea is outside our jurisdiction. You will have to go back to Beit Agron. They will help you."

It is getting on for twelve o'clock. I drive fast. Piety anticipates the Sabbath (and the Israelis confine themselves to a 36 hour weekend) and at Beit Agron everyone who matters has now left. A janitor suggests returning on Sunday morning. So I do. But Major Horowicz, my friend "Alex", has been summoned to a meeting. Nobody else can grant permission to film in Hebron, and I return to England without the precious permit that I had promised to obtain.

In the end we did just manage to film in the Tomb of Abraham, but it took something of a repeat performance of my own endeavours to secure the essential piece of paper. And when I reported at Tantur on my own frustrations, Canon John Wilkinson, the archaeologist, was not at all sympathetic or surprised. "You do realise, don't you," he said, "That you were looking in the wrong place." The real tomb of Abraham, he went on to explain ("although some scholars dispute this") is not amongst those Mameluke colonnades. It is two floors down, in the caves. But whether Isaac's tomb is there, or Jacob's is another question. Certainly the majority of Old Testament scholars doubt whether Isaac was an historical figure. "Very shadowy," my Old Testament tutor, Fr Benedict Green CR, used to say. From a careful reading of the interwoven strands that make up the first five books of the Bible – JEDP in student jargon – Isaac is indeed too good to be true. Crusty old Abraham carries the ring of reality, as certainly crooked Jacob does. Isaac, who makes them grandfather and grandson, makes the story too neat.

As successive patriarchs, they give Judaism a whiff of Trinitarianism that is of some comfort to Christians when they seek to talk of "One God . . . Three Gods". But it is all too pat to be true. Jews may look back to Abraham, as Christians, via them, and Muslims, via Ishmael do. But then the Jewish story effectively starts with Moses, and with Exodus. Genesis just sets the scene. The essential Jewish experience is what Chesterton calls their "monomaniac monotheism", and that stems from Moses, not from Abraham. The Authorised Version gives those who at a tender age first venture, unguided into its pages, some frisson of this monomania. For there in the third chapter of Exodus, by the burning bush the text suddenly leaps into capitals with the words I AM. They are the essential Jewish revelation. They are what is too holy to be spoken. They are the words that we anglicise now as Jahweh, though Jehovah had a good run. For what if anything those words mean is shall-be-was, the eternal other who alone can say "I am".

St. John's gospel afforded pretext for Christian antisemitism, and also provided faithful Judaism with its warrant for the charge of blasphemy. For scattered through his text are the seven "I am's" put into the mouth of Jesus: "the light of the world, the door, the good shepherd, the true vine, the way, the resurrection and the life". A human being is actually the revelation of God: "to the Greeks foolishness, to the Jews blasphemy," as Paul sardonically comments. Some six centuries after this claim a man called Mohammed (blessed be his name) got up from his business, went to Ethiopia to learn what he could from the Christians there about the one true God, and came back and through the suras of the Koran revealed the final message of Allah. The one true god may not be too easily found at the tomb of Abraham.

IV

In the Name of –
   In what name do I pray,
   Jerusalem, today?
Abrahamoff?

Your Ishmael,
   Was your forced slave-girl's son,
   His progeny homespun,
Not Israel.

Isaac came after
   When you were far too old,
   Love in your blood run cold
To Sarah's laughter.

And Jacob then,
   The crooked wheeler-dealer
   Is his the name for Selah,
Old Dad of men?

      Peoples of Abraham,
        Princes of Israel,
          Can you together dwell
      Demands I AM?

5

Where There is No Peace

Shalom! Israel insists on welcoming and saying goodbye to its visitors with the ancient greeting. Salaam – the Arabic form – is not very different. Between Israeli and Arab, peace waits to be conceived.

Peace is written deep into the religious traditions of all three monotheistic traditions. That great Jewish contribution to religion, Sabbath, Shabbat, is its most ancient beacon. The notion that almighty God ceases from activity every seventh day inserts a pause into the rhythm of life. Man is naturally active, naturally competitive, and ever since Cain slew Abel behind competion lurks the shadow of war. Otherwise defined only by negatives, the cessation of hostilities, cold war, *detente* and so on through dozens of diplomatic half-truths, from Sabbath peace enjoys positive sanction. The working week is the price that the sons of Adam pay for their fall from grace. Its climax as the first stars appear on Friday evening redeems it from drudgery. "The Sabbath is made for man," Jesus is recorded as saying, "not man for the Sabbath". For Sabbath enables man to bask in God's reflected glory, and regularly through the changing seasons to enjoy a day that honours God and so lets man share his honour.

Peace, however is not the loudest message of the Bible. Yet for the ancient Israelites, and those who today bind on their phylacteries and seek to follow them, under the umbrella of Sabbath peace huddles from a God of war. The *Torah*, those first five books of the Bible, offers no shrine for peace. The mighty unnameable God is mighty in battle. Without compunction, his waves drown the pursuing Egyptian army. Jebuzites, Perusites and the rest of the unfavoured inhabitants of the land of Canaan are offered no quarter. God is a god of battles. It is left to the prophets, out of the horror of exile, to pipedream of peace. The lion shall lie down with the lamb, and every man shall be at peace under his own figtree. Through such glimpses Isaiah and others recognise the indissolubility of peace. Absence of war is not enough. Somehow the whole of creation has to learn to live in idyllic harmony.

Nor did Jesus, according to the records, speak peace as an easy option. "I came not to bring peace but a sword." "My peace I give unto you, not as the world gives . . ." But then "Peace be unto you, and he breathed on them." The gospels offer no obvious mandate. In the writings of Paul, too, peace is subordinate. In his list of Christian virtues in his letter to the Galatians, peace is third to love and joy. To the Ephesians Paul urges that their feet be shod with the preparation of the gospel of peace, but it is the last item in the armour of light. His most quoted reference embeds itself in a familiar form of blessing; "The peace of God, which passeth all understanding, keep your minds and hearts in the knowledge and love of God . . ." Worn smooth by repetition, the formula yields little meaning. How can peace keep love? Surely it should be the other way round. It has to be said that in the New Testament peace leads a shadowy half life.

"Kate Butler" is a Mennonite. Her blond hair dragged back into a no-nonsense bun to reveal her full-beaming face, this Canadian in her mid-thirties is dedicated to peace. For little more than pocket money she works in the Mennonite Mission, opposite the Ambassador hotel in the diplomatic quarter that flanks Mount Scopus. By word of mouth she attracts a dozen interested visitors to join her unofficial minibus tour of the new settlements. She prefaces the tour with a careful briefing. "If we are stopped, say you are my friends." She has no licence. So under the stream of her passionate explanation, her flock sets forth on a morning's circuit of the city. Indeed what she has to show horrifies the sensitive. First stop is by the new bypass to the Jericho road, which slashes its way through the northern ridge, and which, she relates, Mayor Kollek refused to open. So, with its mounting tale of hilltop dominance, the tour continues. We are issued with maps showing the settlements, and urged not to try and take them through Israeli customs. We see a Palestinian homestead cut off from its fields by slicing new road. We observe an industrial estate, ten miles north from the city centre, within "annexed Jerusalem", lapping the city limits of the Arab twin towns of Al Bireh and Ramallah. We are taken on a detour to view a house destroyed by Israeli marauders, not yet brought to justice. We deviate to salute an isolated Arab smallholding, whose acres were terraced with fifty per cent financial support from the Mennonites, just in time to establish possession under still extant Ottoman law. We wheel through Geet Evron and other new north western architecture, and we note the solar panels. So we pave our way south to the largest bulwark of them all, Gilo. Here 25,000 homes swoop round a ridge in four storied swags, and only a discreet sign marking as "private property" a tiny triangle in the Peace Park at the end of the bluff hints at the last redoubt of the dispossessed owners. Ms Butler tells us what happened. The Palestinian landowner was offered exiguous compensation. For most of the land he accepted it. Then for what remained he was offered an even lower price. He refused it, and dug in. So round him, on land to which his acquiescence he can no longer claim legal title, stands this stone curtain of revette. Within the designated park, he clings proudly to his last roods.

Elsewhere in Gilo our guide pointed out others who cling. Under the shadow of one parabolic block stands one eight-by-eight-by-eight cott. "Cott" for all its archness has to do, since, as was demonstrated, in the one week that the occupier slipped away to deal with other affairs, the second room of her property was razed to the ground. The very stones were used to build a mini Berlin wall on her ground. We saw the old lady, obstinate and shawled, tending her precious garden. If she was an Anna, 84 years widowed, we soon found our Simeon, the old man in his Red Cross tent pitched over against Tantur. Yet after a morning of this propaganda, and its clear evidence, the realisation came that fundamentalists of one side are as counterproductive as those of the other. Yes, it was tempting to draw comparisons with South Africa. Yes, one's heart bled in the Palestinian cause. But, oh my! How in this conflict over a small piece of ground, can any protagonists claim themselves dedicated to peace?

"Allilu Allah . . . Allah akbar . . ." Across the Judean uplands the unprincipled wind carries the muezzin's recorded cry. Islam says nothing about peace. It calls for submission.

Take off your shoes. Take off your shoes, and enter any mosque, take them off at Highbury and enter the warehouse that Yusef Islam (once Cat Stevens) has made his sanctum.

Any stranger, oblivious to circumstance, might be forgiven for supposing himself in the presence of a Whitechapel Jewish tailor, around 1900 CE. A more sensitive visitor, relieved to find no holes in his socks, realises that the man who fifteen or twenty years ago was making a fortune out of "Bridge over troubled water" is now through and through a servant of the prophet (blessed be his name). There is a great clarity about him. For all the nervousness, the improbability of the setting, Yusef Islam comes across – no, is – a man of peace. He radiates it, he has it, he embodies it. The words of the Suras, shorter than the New Testament, and so much more gnomic, may not offer textual critics a blueprint for peace. To stumble up against a Cockney who displays it, unaffectedly, and clearly knows how to market it, numbs intelligence. It is a matter of accepting that Abu Deedat, from Durban, is indeed the man with a message for our times, and for bowing in receipt of two of his videos. It is a matter, also, for remembering, that the informed Muslims of the Islamic Cultural Centre in the Regents Park Mosque, ever so gently express caution: Yusef Islam is more Muslim than the Muslims, they whisper.

Then is peace a red herring? Three monotheistic religions, step-cousins of one another, have for 3,000 years, or 2,000, or 1,400, evolved systems in which "peace" holds a subordinate place. Groups of them give peace prominence, as much as to say this is the real message of our religion, and all those who war in its name are less than perfect. Israel patents Shalom; Quakers institutionalise peace ("christen" would presume to ritual that they eschew) and avatars cry "salaam". In practice, no religion dare put peace too high on its list of priorities; for in doing so it negates its own claim to the whole truth. Under the skirts of "peace" creeps tolerance, and to believers, tolerance is anathema. "The frontiers of faith are patrolled by the mean in spirit" (Colin Thubron), and it is they who dominate religion.

The world lives under the terrible shadow of nuclear winter and every public figure and private person wants to claim allegiance to peace. The common expectation is that religions should be loudest in that claim. Their business is to reconcile man to God. They each talk of God, in similar if irreconcileable terms, as one who cares for the well-being of the world that he makes, and for its inhabitants. Logic would suggest that peace should enjoy a central place on their platforms. It does not. Amongst the Jews of contemporary Israel, orthodoxy is more at home with the hawks. The doves roost amongst the secular left wing. Peace as a political soft-option owes nothing to that religion. Amongst Christians too there is a similar ambivalence. At Christmas the word goes out "Peace on earth, goodwill towards men". It is more accurately translated, unsmiling scholars tell us, as "to men of goodwill", as much as to say demonstrate your goodwill first and then you may be entitled to enjoy the fruits of peace. Yet it is only minorities of Christians-Quakers and Mennonites and a scatter of others, who make peace central to their profession of belief. As to Muslims, peace is low on their agenda. "No first strike" is certainly a central article of belief, but there is no Islamic equivalent to the peace movements that sometimes infiltrate Christianity and invoke its name.

All this is extraordinary. It is particularly extraordinary for Christians. In everyday parlance, being "Christian" means behaving in a way which everyone thinks other people mostly fail to do, and assume that on the whole they do themselves ("but I don't go to church, mind"). Being "Jewish" and being "Muslim" carry no such unctuous supercargo. The nearest public assertion that kindness knows no credal boundaries is in the Red Crescent and the Red Star. When it comes to humanitarianism, very properly neither Jews nor Muslim let the Red Cross pretend that Christians have a monopoly. Beyond that, peace is an orphan.

Beyond it further, religions are two-faced about peace because in their name come so many wars. The present catalogue suffices: Northern Ireland, Southern Lebanon, Iran and Iraq are only the most persistent cesses of war that one side or both wage in the name of one of the three related religions. For all their vaunting, neither Judaism nor Christianity nor Islam can crown peace. Perhaps they do not need to.

For the everyday concept of peace is far from that perfect state which prophets foresaw and to which the pious aspire. All three religions fasten upon the sinful state of man. All three more or less claim to provide a total means of life, and all carry a this-worldly component. So peace has no place at their high table, or at least not common-or-garden peace. Each religion in its different way relegates peace to a world beyond. In Judaism, it beckons from the end of the rainbow, that first sign of God's covenant that he would not again destroy mankind. In the Christian tradition, there is to come a thousand years of peace on earth when Christ is to reign. In Islam, peace is an oasis with an ever rippling stream and lovely damsels in attendance. It lies firmly beyond the grave of this world's hopes.

That is not to dismiss peace to the realm of fantasy. To a Jew, every utterance of "Shalom" is in part a prayer: may peace come; "Shalom Shabbat" is the most precious greeting of the week; may Sabbath usher in peace on its coat-tail. Christianity, in turn, seeks to keep peace on earth. "Christ will come again to judge the living and the dead" declare its ancient and regularly repeated creeds. The belief that on this earth rather than elsewhere all good things will come to fruition is fossilised in Christian doctrine. It stands at the climax of canonical scripture, and nobody in the Christian main stream dare tamper with its place in the canon, but it is left to the fringes of Christianity to trumpet the belief. Prophets arise to declare that the end is nigh, and the bulk of the Christian world leaves them to it. What matters far more to most Christians is the belief that somehow, patiently, God is in control of history.

By contrast, in war time they like to have him on their side. Islam can afford to place peace in paradise because it is not afraid to honour war. War, in defence of the faith, is enjoined upon every faithful Muslim. Peace therefore has no claim on a central place in Islam's understanding of this world. It belongs in Paradise. Both Jews and Christians today have to feel the force of that Islamic doctrine. Judaism has never set enormous store by life after death. In the Jewish Bible it is a shadowy doctrine, only emerging to prominence in the later writings, that lie outside the hallowed canon. To Christianity, it is central: "if Christ be not raised, then is our faith vain". Yet with the decline in this century of a vivid belief in hell and eternal damnation, heaven wilts too. Correctly clerics will maintain it in their compass of preaching, especially just before Christmas when, unseasonably, advent draws attention to these matters. There is little colour to the idea of damnation, without the lurid flames of hell to set it off. For Islam the belief in the life to come is still central and to be a Muslim and not at every moment contemplate the world to be is not to be a Muslim. A Muslim apologist such as Gai Eaton insists that this lively belief in Paradise is one of the main distinctions between Islam and Christianity. When a Christian protests that it is the core of Christian belief, he pooh-poohs that. "You Christians don't live and breath Paradise the way we Muslims do," he insists. A Christian who sits somewhere within the centre of today's western tradition has to concede his point. We do not, as George Herbert did "live each day as if our last". Whatever Christian protestations, the faith today is generally presented as about this world. For bonus points there is heaven to come, but don't go by pie-in-the-sky.

★   ★   ★

"The Third way" is the title of a collection of short pieces by the Palestinian lawyer Raja Shehaddeh. Neither collaboration nor blind hate, the third way for an Arab living under Israeli military occupation is *Sumud*, acceptance; and Raja Shehaddeh proclaims himself *Samad*, accepting. Lincoln's Inn trained, and in his 30s, Raja is a member of his father's law practice in Ramallah. He conducts his profession in an unprepossessing set of offices at 26, Main Street, on the first floor up a flight of steep stairs. Down it his assistant is escorting a blind man who has just been to see about his rights. In the general office a young woman types away on an elderly machine. Raja's office at the end of the corridor smells of law. Round the walls are tomes of law reports, English and Arabic. He sits behind a large desk, cluttered with sets of documents bound in pink tape. He waves his guest to a worn leather seat.

He is impassioned, warm, ever so slightly nervous. Anything to do with television, and he has to be very careful. Any reader of his moving, beautifully written book, is sensitive to that. One of its most painful chapters describes how he took a manuscript to the International Committee of Jurists in Geneva, waiting till the last moment for his visa, never certain till he was safely in the arms of Swissair that he would accomplish his mission.

His book was published in the name of Law in the Service of Man (LSM). An enterprise ten doors down the street that till recently he chaired, L.S.M. shelters under the International

Committee of Jurists. As an individual, a practising lawyer in occupied Samaria, he cannot.

The cases that Raja Shehaddeh fights have to do, almost all, with expropriation: An owner of an orchard cut off from his wells by a new road, without any pretence of consultation, the hard-luck stories of illegal, often brutal, eviction, these are Raja Shehaddeh's bread and marg. For all the distinction of his firm, and his father's impressive reputation, he gives no hint of prosperity. "Of course I could do much better in Jordan; I could even practice in England. But, he is *Samad*, and he stays. Often he loses his cases, overwhelmed by the odds that are stacked against him. Sometimes he wins, The Israeli establishment may condemn his book without reading it; but they let it be published, in Hebrew as well as in Arabic; and he stays.

It is hard to resist the comparison with South Africa. How does he rate Desmond Tutu's Nobel Peace Prize? And it is only then that he mentions that he attended the World Council of Churches Assembly in Vancouver, in 1983, and met Tutu there; and, yes, he is a Christian. He has a close friend, Jonathan Kittab, another lawyer, another Christian. Kittab wears his faith on both sleeves. Raja Shehaddeh prefers to keep his up one. He has, after all, Muslim as well as Christian clients. To parade his faith would risk isolating half his clientele, and they need him every bit as much.

In his book he describes his friendship with "Enoch", Canadian Jewish Psychiatrist from Tel Aviv. Yes, really, Henry, they are friends, and were in the end happy to be filmed together, when "Enoch" revealed his true identity. It was easier for "Enoch" to come and see him than it is for him to go and see "Enoch". His car bears the blue numberplates and that identifies him as from Ramallah. "Enoch", with the yellow plates of Israel (ya boo, Hitler) can drive anywhere without fear of molestation at the frequent check points.

And is *Sumud* peace? No, of course not. There is a state of war. The West Bank is under military occupation. Without some resolution there is no prospect of peace. *Sumud* is the "third way" response to the situation. Anybody who supposes that "peace studies" is an appropriate label for defending the Palestinian cause misuses language. In a state of suppressed hostilities, *Sumud* is something else. It is the realistic response to the wickedness of the world.

At the offices of JRM all this patient realism is confirmed. There works Emma Playfair, an English lawyer of about 30, happy to earn a living in this cause. She produces pamphlet after indicting pamphlet, and doubts whether a visitor will be interested in such minutiae, and speaks uneasily of the cases she takes up. The pamphlets themselves make sombre reading. One is a detailed account of road plans for east-west highways at fifteen mile intervals across Samaria, that are intended to latch the Jordan valley to the seacoast and yoke the Palestinian uplands. A village cut off from its grazing by the swooping bypass that offers no connection, a set of watercourses that make the slopes fruitful destroyed, these are the facts that the pamphlet sets out. One is cautioned not to attempt to take out such incriminating material through Israeli customs. Ms Playfair is an Englishwoman; she has her British passport. She can come and go unimpugned; so far. She makes no secret of the risks she takes, and no way does she see her activities as an advancement to her career. At the only surviving decent restaurant in Ramallah (the rest have closed due to lack of business) she orders in confident Arabic. The restauranteur appreciates her and her custom. This she explains, if you haven't noticed, is a beleagured people. But her name is Playfair, and unlike her passionate coeval, Kate Butler, she is appreciative of the Israeli claims. They have a lien on the country, they have done far more with it than ever the Arabs did. They do make it flow with milk and honey. It is easy to understand the sense of holy triumph with which Israel greets its returning sons, and to appreciate their delight. BUT. There are other people here too; they also have their inheritance, and their claims. They are not Jordanians, however glad they are to clutch their Jordanian passports. They are Palestinians. Law in the Service of Man is a carefully chosen title. Peace. Raja Shehaddeh leaves to his friend Jonathan Kittab a militant proclamation of Christian faith. He keeps his quiet, at least in his office. "They cry peace when there is no peace". For religious people with a tender conscience, "peace" is a seductive word. The Christians of CND, for example, should shame their fellow believers who lurk on the sidelines. The trouble is that peace, like other great words, has been captured. Just as "Christian" is captured by evangelical fundamentalists who dismiss all their fellow Christians as under judgment, so "peace" has been captured by the outrunners of Moscow. It is a hard word to reclaim. To deny its central place is to risk being labelled intolerant, worse still, a warmonger. Any degree of scepticism with those who cry peace earns an uncomfortable rebuke. It is tantamount to denying the essence of the faith. It is to align oneself with the forces of war.

Can a Christian take refuge in the ambiguity of the gospels? "I came not to bring peace but a sword" . . . "My peace I give unto you" . . . "the peace that passeth all understanding" . . . And what can a Jew a Muslim, do? Somewhere all three religious traditions do recognise that peace cannot be identified with constant armistice. War memorials to that horror now nearly beyond living memory, the Great War, mark it as running from 1914–1919. History books, and Remembrance Sunday, remind us of 11/11/1918, and that is the year we recognise. It took the following year to produce the peace treaty of Versailles, and the horrors that from its injustice erupted so soon afterwards. Always we live between the urgency for armistice and the long painful business of agreeing peace. By the token of Versailles, we have not yet achieved the end of the Second World War. Religions, by their very nature, take the long view. They are more in the business of a conclusive peace treaty than of an armistice. What people want is armistices. Religion cheats itself when it totally sides with that desire, for it denies its own perspective.

In the process, religion opens itself to the jibes of unbelievers. It does not like doing so; hence all the fudges. Jews cry "Shalom!", Christians proclaim peace on earth, and Muslims say Salaam. Religion needs to recognise its own imperfections, and its inability to promise peace now.

Peace was all very well when it was the *Pax Brittanica*. It can claim a forty-year track record of sorts as the *Pax Americana*. With experts totting 150 wars since 1945 somewhere round the globe, that Pax wavers; but then a century (1815–1914) of Pax Britannica had its tally of colonial wars of conquest and gunboat diplomacy, so there is not too much joy in seeing greater pax under the Union Jack than under the Stars and Stripes. The only consolation is that the two in turn kept major war off decent doorsteps.

For Christians (or even the courteous Muslims who come from Regent's Park to engage in Rainbow dialogue) to accept the Jewish reading of their mid-twentieth century history certainly calls for revision of their earlier triumphalism. "The world for Christ in our generation," proclaimed the heroic "Cambridge Seven", around the turn of the century, and set forth to achieve it. Mission languishes, as the flags come down. Instead, languid British Christianity has to come to terms with the growth, across the third world, of indigenous Christian forms that, like the political systems under which they flourish, cast off what they were taught from Westminster. These forms march against the spread of Islam: in Africa, in the East Indies, in the Indian sub-continent, the two scarred militant monotheitic faiths battle under new uniforms. They are a long way from Oswiecin, or from the Jewish Independent State of Israel.

A long way, but still in the same world: the return of the Falasha from Ethiopia in 1984 set the world alight as another example of Israeli daring. There are still almost as many Jews in India as there are in Israel. In the Soviet Union there are more; and in the United States. Jewry is also worldwide. Christian or other sceptics who hesitate to see 20th century history written in terms of holocaust and Israel have to allow that Judaism, too, has place as a world religion. For all that Christians secretly want to put down Jewry as a middle European phenomenon, that has found fresh life in the Holy Land, that plays false to facts. Not to dwell upon the Sephardim, from Spain and Portugal and (subsequently) Holland and England, the Oriental Jews all across Asia eastwards from Jerusalem, are the third ingredient that the state of Israel aspires to bring home. After all, Israel needs its workforce.

A look at the whole globe pushes holocaust and the establishment by its survivors of the state of Israel slightly off centre stage. Whatever peace is, is it not to be written only in those challenging terms. The terrible event and the triumphant one were episodes in a wider drama. Peace cannot be written by accepting the Ashkenazi interpretation of events. Jew, Christian and Muslim focus piety on Jerusalem, a city since 1967 occupied in its entirety by the Independent Jewish State of Israel.

Together the three related monotheistic religions straddle the world. Christianity and Judaism, these past four hundred years, have shown most energy in the North Atlantic world. Islam has not. Its mainspring has been, till recently, the middle east from which it sprang. The holocaust and the foundation of the state of Israel were North Atlantic phenomena. Islam stands to remind us that this is not the only perspective. Israel's creation brought flocking the Jews of the Arab world, and hardened the boundaries of hate. Their return (*aliyah*) leavened the immigration of the survivors of the Nazi attempt to exterminate Jewry. It is their return, not in 1948, but over the four decades since, that gives fuller colour to history.

V

Up and down the cliffs of Cornwall,
   Bearing lanterns, rode the sharks
To lure to death the stormstruck gunwale,
   Spurious shelter for those barques.

Jogging pinpoints coaxed them shorewards,
   There Atlantic turmoil'll cease;
Lights are only crafty stewards
   Of destruction and decease,
To lure the unsuspecting leewards.
   And they'll scramble for their booty,
Kegs and coils that excise craved;
   Seaman who evaded duty,
Lucky if their lives are saved.

   Hallowed strand, Levantine littoral,
Israel urges sons ashore;
   "Shalom!" seductively hospitable
Calls its immigrants and more:

   Come from your diaspora, Jews,
Join our kibbutzim and caelidhs
   It's not difficult to choose,
Well soon make of you Israelis.
   If you thought you feared our Jahweh,
Not to worry, God is dead.
   Immigrate, be Jewish our way,
Zion be your god instead.

6
O Wild West Wind

"No", said the husky voice over the phone, "I can't see you today. I'm going to Haifa".

"Tomorrow, Wednesday?"

"I shan't be back till Wednesday evening".

"Thursday then?"

"Well, you can certainly come and see me, but you may not want to. Thursday is my silent day."

"Then why don't you let me drive you to Haifa today?"

"Oh certainly, come on over," and she gave unusually precise directions how to find her street. They led to an old Turkish village called Manahat, about four miles south west of the city centre on the Gaza road. "Third house on the left, more or less, but just ask," she had said. Somebody had let me have a poster with her photograph on, and it was just as well. Bemused by this tangle of old cottages I waved it at the first woman, a rather dark skinned old thing in the street.

"Eh bien, Shelley," she said, and proceeded in fluent French to give me detailed instructions. But then, of course, she was a Jew from Morocco; as Shelley, too, prides herself on being, only nine generations back. For Shelley Elkayam, poet, aged 28, is Sephardi.

That has to be the first thing to say about her.

It did not come out at once. Scrambling over the rocks in her backyard, I knocked at the door.

"Entrez", said the husky voice cheerfully, "I'm dressing. Hillel, find Christopher some coffee". It was a tiny place, sparsely furnished, and the clouds of incense pervaded. From out of them emerged a docile young man in jeans. "Hillel wants to come to Haifa too", Shelley called from out of her shower. On the windowsill beside me was a framed photograph of some Guru, a set of prayer-beads and a fifty-dollar note. It was her shrine, apparently, and I hesitated to lodge my drink there. "Oh, don't worry", said Shelley, rolling the phrase round her mouth like Marlene Dietrich, and she emerged in a robe from the shower. "It's not a shrine. No, I don't worship the guru, nor the almighty dollar. God is who matters, his spirit. Tell me what you think of this poem of mine; Hillel recorded the musical backing for it".

"It's called 'The Song of the Architect'".

She put on a cassette, and there was herself on tape, reciting her Hebrew lines, to percussion and the touch of a flute. I listened and politely admired.

"No but seriously, what do you think?"

"But I don't understand Hebrew".

"Does that matter? It's poetry; here, look at this Dutch translation; and there's one in English. Tell me if you think that's good".

It wasn't, and I said so. The Dutch seemed much sturdier. "Yes, that's what Gerrit told me. Will you find me somebody who can translate Hebrew into English? And, tell me, which shoes should I wear?"

In the photograph that I had been carrying Shelley appeared sharp, thin-faced, with angular features and a hard look. In the flesh she is altogether rounder, almost dumpy. Everytime she laughs, up goes her chin, and the laughter disappears down her throat. Only when she smokes and is self-consciously holding an audience does she display something of the angular poise of that publicity photo.

Hillel was bundled into the back of the little car, and I started the engine. "Wait a moment", said Shelley reproachfully, "we haven't prayed yet, and she put on her poetry voice to invoke divine blessing on our journey.

"Amen", I added, glad to make that much contribution. She rounded on me. "Do you mean it? 'Amen' is a very solemn thing to say. For of course she believed in God. Of course prayer is important. The synagogue? Pfui! Leave that to Ashkenazim!"

With Hillel being fed cigarettes and cherries to keep him quiet, the three hour journey to Haifa gave Shelley plenty of time to present her philosophy of life.

"My father chose the name Shelley for me. In Hebrew it means the peaceful one. He did not know that it was the name of an English poet. My mother wanted to call me Rachael . . ."

"Mourning for her children, at Rama", I chipped in.

"Yes, it is a sad name; but I have it too. I prefer Shelley. Names are very important. What does yours mean?" She mused over the Greek derivative of Christopher, the carrier of Christ. "That is a very heavy load. Can you bear it?" But she was more concerned to tell me about Elkayam. "It means 'going with God'". "That takes some bearing too".

It is a very old Sephardi name. I go with God, and I love the world, and all God's people in it".

"Including the Ashkenazi?"

"Pfui! I'd like one of your cigarettes".

She had never been to England. She had been to Canada, to Kenya, and three times she had been in Holland. The first time she spent five months there. Now she is regularly invited and sponsored as a young Israeli poet to attend the gatherings of Poetry International in Rotterdam. The freedom of Dutch life amongst the poets and artists suited her very well. "But they are surprised to find a Jew who believes in God as I do. One God, your god and mine. Yes, he's male and female, certainly, but a bit more man, I think. But then I'm a woman, don't worry".

And had she broadcast? Yes, once, reluctantly. The Israeli broadcasting service tracked her down when she came back from Rotterdam, and wanted to interview her. "I didn't want to go. They only want people who praise Israel. The others said I must go. In the end I went and said what I thought. They cut most of it."

Shelley Elkayam is World Vice-President of the Youth Section of the World Conference for Religion and Peace. It sounds like a ponderous title for someone so effervescent. "But I tell you, Christopher, that is how we began to get the Falashas out of Ethiopia". By this stage it is possible to believe anything.

She goes on to describe how the previous summer she had been as a delegate at the WCRP assembly in Nairobi. As Ammerdown had confirmed, the WCRP, whose title could make it anything from a fellow-travelling to a Moonie front organisation, is a respectable organisation with its headquarters in Lausanne. Its notepaper lists admirable patrons drawn from a global list of the great and the good. At Nairobi a curate from Rochester and Shelley had taken the initiative to form a youth section, and secured the approval of their elders. Fortified by that achievement, Shelley in Nairobi met a Sudanese diplomat, and with him began to discuss the growing famine in Ethiopia and in particular, the question of the Falashas.

"Our government took no notice", she went on, scornfully, and then described her lobbying up and down the corridors of the Knesset. She quoted, as if she could provide chapter and verse for it, the familiar tag attached to any American Jew returning to live in Israel. "Did I leave Brooklyn to live with a lot of schwarzers?"

So her Sephardic disdain for the ruling Ashkenazim comes out. They have all returned to Israel – *aliyah* is the Hebrew word for it – from north of the Alps or across the Atlantic. They simply do not know how to live as the peoples of the Mediterranean world have long learned to live, with a sunburnt indifference to colour. Consequently, runs her argument, from the beginning Israel has been in two minds about encouraging the mass return of the black Jews.

"They make all this fuss about the four million Jews in the Soviet Union. What about the rest. They don't really want them swarming in here. They would be swamped".

Nonetheless, according to Shelley's account, the Israeli government in the end decided to retrieve the Falasha, and mounted their prodigious secret airlift. Subsequent events have certainly proved her right in one respect. In July 1985 the Falasha mounted their protest march to Ben Gurion international airport, threatening to decamp to Ethiopia unless the orthodox rabbinate gave up its insistence that all the men should be ritually circumcised in order to attest to their validity as Jews. The Israeli government had to climb down. The problems that faced the early Christian Apostles are still around. Abraham circumcised Ishmael before he circumcised Isaac. Christian men alone are free to interpet the first patriarch's sign of faith in a spiritual way.

Hillel had been dozing gently in the back of the car. As we came under the lee of Mount Carmel and into Haifa it was time to rouse him. He wanted to be dropped off near the university. Then Shelley explained (previously she had not bothered to do so) that he was simply a man she knew who ran a disco company. She was on her way to visit her parents, who lived in a new town somewhere to the north of the city. On we drove.

However hospitable the reception, a non-Jewish visitor to a Jewish home is sensitive to the difference. A touch of brassiness about the decor, a slight defensive over-enthusiasm about the welcome, whispers amongst the hosts as they seek to make their visitor comfortable, all hint at estrangement. In the Elkayam's home there was absolutely none of that feeling. Chaim and Clara, her parents, even her schoolgirl sister had an immediate easiness about them. Allowing that they had had a phone call to warn them they did not fuss in the least to find an unknown Englishman driving their daughter home, though we had (to my embarassment) kept them waiting till four o'clock for their midday meal. Even the uncertainties about which plate to use, which fork, that are the lot of a guest in strange surroundings, did not seem to matter in the least. They gave the impression of feeling very settled, and Chaim, clearly proud of his daughter, volunteered his Moroccan origins eight generations back. "We belong here," he said. "Long before we were Israelis we were Palestinians."

Clara made no such territorial claim. She was Macedonian. By present frontiers her mother was Greek, her father Bulgarian. Her first language (and Shelley had claimed that she spoke seven) was Ladino. She was the daughter, granddaughter of *dhimmi*, Jews who had lived for generations under the suzerainty of the Ottoman Empire. In her background, the reigning religion was Islam. There were some Christians around, as well, come to think of it, but it was the minaret, and the call of the muezzin, that set the tone for the day, rather than the clang of church bells. To be brought up in those surroundings as a young Sephardi Jewess was not a matter of religion. She did not recall her father relying for strength on the synagogue. Being Jewish was not religion. It was being Jewish, and the way they cooked. Jewishness only stuck out in 1941 when the Germans came; but they managed to escape to Palestine, and she was glad to be there still.

We were somewhere into a leisurely second course when in walked Boaz. He is the Elkayams' younger son, doing his two years' stint of military service. He was wearing the familiar fatigue drill of the Israeli army. He was doing time, guarding some national shrine or other, somewhere near Jerusalem. It all sounded far too boring to invite the question which shrine. It might have been the Tomb of Abraham, but it wasn't, actually. His older brother Jacov was a regular. Sign on for three years, and there is promise of a commission. He was much nearer home, some forty miles to the north, engaged in the hostilities in the Lebanon. The family hardly ever heard from him, and did not really expect to. Being Jewish is about being Jewish. In the end to be Sephardi is not the point, not now in Israel, anyway.

★   ★   ★

All that Shelley had really come home for was to dump on her mother some foam rubber mattresses, and yards of calico with which to cover them. Clara took this requirement in good heart. So, her daughter had been married, her daughter had been divorced. So it comes, so it goes. Shelley is a lovely girl, and look at all she is doing! Momma is there to sew calico covers round mattresses. Shelley likes to have her friends to stay. They must have something to sleep on. "I'll have them ready for you by Shabbat," she promises.

For at half past five in the afternoon the day is young, and there is yet much to be done. Shelley has been fabricating our programme. Most important, she has to see Waleed.

"Oh, have you made an appointment with him?"

"Don't worry, he knows that it is time we met."

Then, since we are going to Nazareth, why don't we call in at her old kibbutz. It is ages since she saw her ex-husband, and high time to say hello. And there is someone there that I should meet. Alexander Barzel would be just the man for our programme.

Shelley offers to drive. Like all her offers, it is one that brooks no refusal. Like all she does, she drives with alarming verve. Well within the hour, we are driving into the kibbutz.

Kibbutz Kfar Hahoresh is one of the oldest kibbutzim. It was established in the 1930s, during the time of the British mandate. Driving into it in the dark gives only an impression of a gateway between a high hedge. The closely planted prickly pears are now mature and decorative. When they were dug in there, fifty years ago they served as barbed wire. In those pioneering days the first need of any kibbutz was its stockade. In the heart of the Galilee those Jewish settlers were constantly under threat of attack from the Palestinian natives. Police protection from the British mandate was rarely enthusiastic.

Half a century later, and the kibbutz, covering nearly a square mile of a hillside sloping south is more like a well established holiday village that could do with a coat of paint. Narrow tarmac strips, dimly lit, thread their way between a succession of long low wooden hutments. An open square somewhere in the middle of the complex might once have served as a sort of parade ground. Now there are lots of little cars parked on it.

Shelley has forgotten her way to the Barzel's bungalow. She enquires of a passing resident whom she greets like an old friend. Then we find the place, and a man she hardly knows welcomes us into his home as if we were expected old friends. Shelley is content to introduce me, and then skips away to call on Gilead, her ex-husband, and his wife. "Don't worry, we are very good friends."

Mrs Barzel appears, producing coffee and cakes. There is a touch of old Vienna about the room. They are a couple aged about 60, who have lived here for forty years. She does not often leave the kibbutz, it is her life, and soon she retires to her kitchen. So for the better part of an hour there is Alexander Barzel.

Dean of Humanities in the Haifa Technion, and Master Baker, four days a week, Sunday to Wednesday, he drives to Haifa and conducts his teaching programme. On Thursdays and Fridays he bakes not just bread for the kibbutz but for selling throughout Israel as bread to be used in Friday night family seders. Then comes Shabbat. Alexander Barzel is an Orthodox Jew.

He was a baker before he was an academic. "I only started to read when I was forty," he explains nonchalantly, as one might speak of taking up a new hobby in early middle-age. His shelves are lined with books, in German, English and Hebrew; books of philosophy, of history, of social thought, of politics, and a great deal of contemporary serious fiction. These last twenty years, he has clearly caught up on his reading.

His first interest was the philosophy of history. For the sake of good argument, I suggest that Jews really have no sense of history, as process, and ever since the exodus have been living in an extended present. He considers this proposition as an interesting intellectual challenge. On the contrary, he argues, it is the Jews who have given the world history. It is we, he claims, who found its sense of purpose. Who else has shown how to talk of the moral value of events? India certainly never has, none of the ancient civilisations did. What about the Greeks, I suggested, and what about Thucydides? Yes but even Thucydides did not easily see beyond the competing virtues of the city states. He lacked that sense of overruling righteousness. But then, I argued, the Jews have always wanted to focus it all on themselves. That, he replied, is what the Jews are for. That is our destiny.

From history we moved to culture. Here was he, Dean of Humanities in a technical university. Israel was justifiably proud of its technological achievement, in agriculture, in chemicals, even in the military field. What contribution could a Dean of Humanities make in an institution where technology was king? All the undergraduate students, he explained, have to take some courses in humanities. It may be history, it may be art, it may be literature, they can choose; but achievement in those courses counts towards their degree. It is not just a little diversion for them.

And religion? Oh, yes certainly. The philosophy of religion was his best attended class. No, of course it was not his business to give instruction in orthodox Judaism. That was the business of the home, of the rabbis. His business was to encourage his students to have an informed understanding of their religion. "Religion" was the word that Alexander Barzel kept using, never "faith".

Yes, there were a few non-Jews among his students; several Christians, one or two Muslims perhaps. What then did he make of our enquiry into "One God . . . Three Gods"? He was sceptical. A religion is a religion. They go very deep. It is no use trying to mix them. In Haifa we have the world centre of the Ba'hai, with that lovely golden-domed temple. Ba'hai, no. A hundred and fifty one years ago they thought that you could create one true religion by stirring all the others in a pot. You cannot make a good loaf of bread by mixing in every ingredient that you can think of. The mixture has to be right, it has to be precise, it has to be pure. Otherwise it will never rise and bake properly. It will not be fit for human consumption.

Do you remember Abraham, he went on, and how he entertained angels unawares (which of your writers wrote that very good phrase?). There were three of them, and Abraham told Sarai to bake three loaves of bread, a different one for each of them. From Abraham come each of our three religions. There were three angels, three loaves. Here it is in the Torah, in the book of Genesis. It is a prophecy. If the Lord of the Universe had meant there to be only one religion, Sarai would have been commanded to make only one loaf for them to share; or there would have been only one angel. But not so; three loaves, three angels.

So spoke the Master Baker. When we looked at his diary to see when he might be available to appear in front of our camera, the problems were formidable. One week he would be fully committed to a group of visiting American academics. The next few days he would be back in Jerusalem for meetings. Then he would be back in the kibbutz baking (but was not that just the setting to film him?).

Altogether it was going to be difficult, and in fact we never included him in the programme. Instead Yeheskal Landau zealous young academic who is the moving force in *oz ve shalom* (justice and peace), despite proving elusive in the course of the reconnoitre, did emerge in time to be filmed. Like Alexander Barzel, he represents a point of view that is an essential piece of the jigsaw, that of the committed Jew who knows that Israel has to be open if it is to be human, if it is to survive.

GUTS OF THE CITY

Let us watch the Hilton
as it waxes like a new moon
over the gates of Zion.
Once
you wished for a home
in Yerusalayim.

Now the night is a heart of shadows,
now the heart abstains
but perhaps my soul quivers.
I open my eyes to see
what I already knew
Through the window the entrails of the city
reveal themselves to me.
Guts of the city.

You are asleep. Your spine stiffens. Your breath is hard.
I'll arrive like a knife in the midst of your love.
I'll arrive like a wisp of steam in the mist of your heart.
You will leave
and only what you take with you will be yours.

Now
let us watch the Hilton
as it waxes like a wan moon
over the gates of Zion.

Shelley Elkayam

7
Thou Breath of Autumn's Being

Shelley burst in upon our conversation, all bubbling, and soon whisked me away. "I can't wait to get out of this place," she said, as soon as we were in the car. "It gives me the shivers." This time she forgot to pray as we started our journey; perhaps the previous prayer was still valid.

"Thank goodness I am divorced. Thank goodness I am no longer a kibbutznik. Gilead and that wife of his – oh she is quite a nice girl really – how can they bear to go on living within this compound? It is boring, and they are bored. And that little baby of theirs will never be allowed to get out. I gave him a little present from Holland. One day that may make him want to see the world."

Shelley had been married at nineteen, and for four years lived in this kibbutz. Then she found a pretext to escape on her own to Jerusalem for a few days, and from there her career had taken off. She had no rancour about her marriage, no sign of a scar, no remorse. It was simply a past episode in her life, good enough while it lasted, but thank goodness it was long over.

We were coming into Nazareth, and it was the evening of Lady Day. I was expecting parades, bells, fireworks, a town *en fête*. There was no sign of anything. The only hint of a festal day was the floodlighting that illuminated the ponderous 1900-ish dome of the Roman Catholic cathedral which stands plonk in the middle of the town. Why Nazareth ignored the Feast of the Annunciation was the first question that I wanted to ask Waleed.

For Waleed Khlief is an Arab Christian. In his early fifties, perhaps, his face is drawn in sad lines, that only break into cheer when he enthuses. Again, there is no show of surprise as he greets us at the portal of his home, and leads us across his yard into the house. It is a large parlour, shabbily furnished in an old-fashioned way. In the centre stands a large table, with an oriental rug running across it. There are horsehair sofas against the walls; on a niche stands a plaster statuette of Our Lady, and a rosary. Two girls in their teens are watching the black-and-white television. Waleed pleads with his daughter and her friend to switch off and leave the room, for we have business to discuss.

For, like Shelley, Waleed is a poet, and their meeting is to discuss plans for the forthcoming First Hebrew/Arab poetry festival. The event is Shelley's notion, and in Waleed she has found a willing accomplice. The event is planned for a couple of months' time, in Nazareth, and they are hoping to attract a dozen or more poets to declaim their verses in front of a public audience. "Not just Jews and Christians," Waleed explains, kindly bringing me into the conversation. "We even hope to have a Muslim Professor of Poetry from Nablus!" Nablus and Nazareth are twenty-five miles apart. Between them there is a great gulf fixed, for Nablus, in Samaria, is the most militantly Arab city, and the proposal is nothing if not daring.

Even now, no firm arrangements have been made, and there is much to fix. What place, and, more important, what date? And now there is this possibility of British television. Waleed grows excited. What better way could our film show cooperation between the peoples of different religions? As his enthusiasm mounts, with promises to fix everything, so in my mind the whisper of caution strengthens. For Waleed and Shelley and their companions, it might indeed be marvellous propaganda. It is hard to picture a British television audience equally thrilled. We haggle round the question of English translations of the poems. Waleed knows somebody who could make beautiful renderings. It would be very moving. Shelley is the one to express doubt. Nobody can make good translations of my poems, even from Hebrew, she says, as if that were easier to do.

We agree to adjourn, and to meet towards the end of the evening at the New Grand Hotel. Waleed's daughter's friend is the daughter of the manager, and we shall be welcome there. Meanwhile he will go off and fix things, and he can find us beds if we need them; and he will get one or two others to join us.

Even now, I am naively expectant about seeing the well-to-do Christians of Nazareth celebrating their feast day in the town's leading hotel. When we go in there sometime after ten o'clock the place is empty. They produce a meal for us, which turns out to be with the compliments of the management, and that says something for Waleed's powers of fixing. Some friend of Waleed's has joined us, but contributes nothing to the discussion. Point by merciless point, Shelley spend the time fanning Waleed's crumpled leaves into activity to make the detailed arrangements for the poetry festival. Agreeing to meet again the following Saturday, towards midnight we depart.

"Now," says Shelley, giving instructions to her chauffeur, "we go home." She does not mean to her parents at Quirat Biariq, forty miles away, where I should have slept soundly on one of those pieces of foam rubber mattresses. She means back to Jerusalem, all of 180 miles away via the motorway that runs along the coast.

She is still in dancing mood. I have shown her Sydney Carter's poems, and she responds particularly to "Lord of the Dance". "But that is not Jesus," she says, "it is Shiva" I tell her that Sydney is aware of the connection. "Ah", she says, "if only Solomon had been." Shiva is the Queen of Sheba, she explains. However the Bible explains it, her visit was an offer from Hindu religion to embrace the Hebrew religion in its ample bosom. Solomon refused. So Judaism remains male and infertile. "Shiva," I add, playing her game, "also has to do with good and evil." "Yes, of course," says Shelley, ever one move ahead, "and that too is why Solomon was unwise to refuse her embrace. Ever since God had been punishing Israel for its obstinacy and misunderstanding. Since Solomon, this has never been a united land."

About 3 a.m. I deposit her on her doorstep in Manahat, relieved at the prospect of my welcoming bed in Tantur. No wonder she needs a day of silence on Thursdays.

The following Saturday I am knocking on her door at 6.30 a.m. She is up bright as the lark. "Let's go through the Jordan Valley for a change," she suggests. I suggest the direct route, through Samaria. She quails. For all her claim to be liberated, a Sephardi and a citizen of the world, the old instinct comes out. No Jew, who can possibly avoid it, travels from Jerusalem to the Galilee by the straight road. But I am at the wheel, and unkindly set out on that route. We get as far as Ramallah. Shelley has never been there. She is goose-pimpled with anxiety, so we compromise. Just short of the headquarters of the Israeli military administration, a compound that I have come to know, is a sign of pointing right to Jericho. According to the documentation distributed by Law in the Service of Man, this is another of the new roads that the Israelis are ruthlessly slashing west to east across the Samarian uplands, and it would be interesting to inspect their damage.

After a few hundred yards aggressive concrete gives way to an old strip of tarmac, evidently of British mandate vintage. It is a lyrical road. The highway that the Israelis have carved running down from Jerusalem to Jericho is much too fast and smooth to give a Christian pilgrim a sense of following the hoofprints of the Good Samaritan's donkey. This parallel lane, ten miles to the north, in the early morning opens wondering eyes to the eternal verities of Palestine.

From above the mountains of Moab, in Jordan to the east beyond the rift valley, the majestic sun rises and clears the clouds out of his path. Only in the wadis that run down to the unseen valley below is there still a flooring of early morning mist. Here on these high moors everything is springtime green. We make our way through first one village, a Christian one, with its church bell clanging, and then a couple of miles later through a Muslim one, the minaret silent, since the muezzin has an hour since delivered his dawn call. There we stop, and from the village shop, refresh ourselves with lemonade. Ours is the only traffic in this dawn, and from crest to crest we swoop and soar in silence. A couple of goats trot indignantly out of our way and we catch a glimpse of a Bedouin encampment in a fold of the hills. Then comes the escarpment, and gingerly we wind down through a combe the two thousand feet to the bed of the rift valley.

Already it is hot down here. The sun has evacuated the mist, and begun its long day's tour of duty here. The workers are out in their plantations, with sprinkler and with mattock, and as we head north up the Jordan valley the early sellers are at their pitch by the roadside; boxes of giant tomatoes are their ware.

The Israeli tourist literature warns visitors not to drive east of this road, and there is no turning to tempt us. Yet we are still a hundred feet or more above the valley bed, and the river itself is invisible. Suddenly I am struck by the ploughed patterns in the sand on the right of the road, and as we round a corner there is a high wire fence.

"Jordania," explains Shelley, and explains that the patterns in the sand are a detective device to reveal the footprints of invading terrorists. This beautiful morning landscape is suddenly Berlin, and Israel gives off another whiff of claustrophobia. Shelley says it is her turn to drive, and drives with her usual attack. "We are due in Nazareth at nine," she reminds me. Punctuality has not been one of her marked concerns, and she is accelerating to get beyond this edgy frontier strip.

Well before nine we reach Nazareth, and Waleed is ready for us. For Shelley and himself he has arranged a full working morning's schedule. For me he has made a series of appointments, with people who, assures me, will be absolutely essential for our film. None of them in fact appear in it, and Waleed's timetabling proves optimistic. He has made no allowance for Nazareth's Saturday jam. The old town of Nazareth is Arab, half Muslim, half Christian. On the hillside a mile above stands the new town of Nazareth Illit, which is Jewish. On Shabbat its residents forgo their principles and drive down in their big cars to shop in the Nazareth market. The streets of the old town cannot absorb that influx.

After various appointments, and some missed ones, by noon I arrive as agreed in the Nazareth tourist office. That is our rendezvous. In desultory conversation with the man behind the desk, evidently the office manager, only gradually do I appreciate that his is one of the very important names that Waleed has given me to meet. So to business. And Antoine Shaneen is indeed a person of substance. Arab, devout Roman Catholic, long time secretary of the Nazareth ecumenical comittee and literally responsible for creating the local interfaith committee, this former communist has much to say. His spoken French is most elegant, and with his domed balding head and exquisitely manicured nails, he lacks only a discreet rondel in his lapel to name him some kind of chevalier.

He describes very carefully the political position of the various Christian churches. Certainly the Greek Orthodox have long been loudest in their support of the left. It does not follow that only members of that church vote DFPE. For Arab Palestinian who accept their Israeli citizenship, that party best expresses their detachment from the mainstream of Jewish Israeli politics. Reflecting in how many parts of the world the church stands in opposition to the Communist party, I express some surprise at this alliance. He has his response. What about Sinn Fein in Northern Ireland? But that, I say, is not Communist. No, indeed, but where does its outside support come from? Noraid in the USA. I reply, politely to trump him. And nothing he asks, from the Soviet Union? He has made his point.

So we turn to discussing our television project. He hears me out as I explain my growing feeling that we ought to concentrate on religion rather than on the issue of peace. You mean that you want to filter out people's religious beliefs and detach them from politics, he enquires. And yet you say that you start from the premise that if religion matters at all it is to do with the everyday. And you talk of these students whom you met in Bethlehem, and say that they disappoint you because in no way do they appear to relate their religious beliefs to their present situation. *Tiens, tiens!*

There was a ruthless French logic about his analysis of the problem. On the one hand it had become clear in my mind that for the film to concentrate on peace, meaning the difficulties of the Palestinians under Israeli government, would be to fail in its aim. That was the very sidetrack down which Tantur seemed to be heading, and to that extent failing to fulfil its central purpose. The opposite mistake was to try and treat religion, and religious belief, in a vacuum, and pretend that it had no bearing of the everyday. To do that would be totally false to our conception of the series. How should we steer between them? Did he not think that there was a way of attending to political realities but focussing our attention on religion?

Certainly, *mon ami*, certainly. The way you do it is to take people's religious beliefs as given. Accept what they tell you about them. As far as you can, understand their religious practice, and what their religion means to them. Do not approach their views, whatever your own may be, in a spirit of judgement. The good god makes us as we are, gives us our families and our formation. If some of us are called to peer a little beyond our particular boxes, good. We should not count on others being so called too. Even those of us who are called to peer – perhaps we are by nature a little inquisitive – must remember to belong where we are. Here am I, running this tourist office these twenty years, yes an Arab, a Palestinian, and a public functionary of the Israeli government. That is my situation. And I arrange for the tourists, the pilgrims if you like, to come to this town. They see what they want to see, and it is my business to help them. They do not want to see anything else, and they would not thank me if I tried to show them other than what they expect. If they come in a pilgrim spirit, they come to be satisfied with what they know they can find here.

"But even for the sake of tourism, isn't it part of your business to encourage them to look over the fence?"

Look, my friend, I peer over the fence. So the good god calls me to do; for of course there is only one God. I am also a devout Roman Catholic. Monday was our feast day, and I did not come to the office. I am pious. The office stayed open, naturally. We have tourists to serve. In my view the only way that any of us can hope to find the true god is by being faithful to our own particular tradition; but it does help to be a little bit open, too.

Apologetically, Waleed bursts in, forty minutes behind schedule. Shelley enters a few moments later, banging a goatskin drum that she had just bought. To the embarrassment of Waleed, a respected citizen of Nazareth, she insisted on banging it all the way up the street to the car. Once again, Waleed has made good his ability at arranging things. "I am a poor man," he says, explaining why he cannot himself offer us hospitality. "Poets are poor. But I have good friends." So a friend of his who is an estate agent takes us out to lunch, and explains something of the complexities of buying property in Israel. They do not have building societies. Mortgages are practically unknown. A person with little capital wanting to buy a house must spend hard cash on an empty site; and then with the help of his friends and relations, be ready to build it himself. Building regulations, at least, are not so strict as they are in Britain.

Shelley falls asleep as we set off from Nazareth after lunch. She claims not to have slept for three nights. We are to go back to Kiriat Biariq, to collect the mattresses from her mother. On the way there I am determined to find Revd Elias Chagour. He is the Melchite parish priest of a village called Ibolin, which is not far off our route. Various people had encouraged me to contact him. He is, they assured me, an obvious candidate for the programme. He had written a book called 'Blood Brothers' which had caused quite a stir and been a best-seller. All the bookshops in East Jerusalem have sold out of it. "Try London," was the suggestion.

The book describes his pastorate in an Arab village that has a mixed Christian and Muslim population. It had no school, and he was determined to provide one. It was against Israeli government policy to encourage the further building of church schools. It offended against the law of 1978 which bans missionary activity. Fr Chagour, meanwhile, had the ready support of his parishioners, the Muslims as well as the Christians. Even the local Imam raised no objections. So Fr Chagour set to work with voluntary labour. If that is the way to build a house, it can also be the way to build a school. Each weekend he began recruiting a dozen volunteers. He could hardly keep his activity secret, and the Israeli authorities required names of the volunteers. The subsequent weekend those volunteers would receive official summonses requiring them to present themselves in Haifa, on some pretext or other. No matter. There were plenty more volunteers where they came from. So, eventually, under the beetling frowns of authority, Fr Chagour built his school.

It was not too difficult to find. At the beginning of the village, with Shelley still asleep, I picked up a village lad. He actually guided me to Fr Chagour's house, but there his housekeeper gave us directions to the school. It turned out to be an orphanage as well, with a dozen urchins playing under the stern eye of Sister Joseph. She said that Fr Chagour had gone to Nazareth for the day. No matter; later we spoke on the phone, and he has plenty to say in our film.

Shelley's mother had just finished making the mattress covers; she clearly had no inhibitions about doing needlework on the Sabbath. Shelley received them gratefully, and Chaim gave me two large lemons from his tree. Shelley took over the wheel and we set off back to Jerusalem.

"Tell me more about this Bishop Montefiore of yours," she said suddenly. "He is Sephardi, yes." I told her a good deal.

And then she recited this new poem of hers, The Song of the

Architect, and we were away into an underworld of freemasonry and secret signs.

"You know, Christopher, to us Sephardim the Kabbala has always been very important. Very important. Now don't say it is hocus-pocus. My friends in Holland say that, and I will not have it. It points the way to secret knowledge, the way to the spirit of the universe."

There were several miles of her thoughts on the matter, as we drove back down the coastal motorway. "And so you see," she concluded triumphantly, "I am beginning to think that if we want to find one god, three gods, we must study the mysteries."

I did not want to go down these dark alleys, and we parted on disappointingly cool terms. But there was some errand that took me to see her next morning, before I left for London, and she makes a substantial contribution to the series.

TRIO

See you in another place, Joe.
In the Norwegian deserts, the Sahara
perhaps.
I'll come in a coat of many colours.
And the sun
forges the flesh of longing

Into a naked dialogue
arid and
bare

Another place, Joe.
Crystal-clear in the woods of the fallen snow.
I'll be calling you another name.
It's later than we think, said I.
Now she is weighed
and measured
clear and void of prayer.
An orange moon rises over the forest
it will wane till tomorrow
its skies trembling less

Shelley Elkayam

8
Here Stand I

Shelley's religious adventurism leads into mystic marshes. After that first long day with her it was reassuring to have made an appointment of a very different kind. For next morning I was due to meet Professor Leibowicz. "Oh, you are not seeing him!" was the conventional chorus. For this old scribe, with his six earned academic doctorates covering the arts and the sciences, is notorious throughout Israel for his eccentric views. At the age of 82, he regularly accepts invitations to address public audiences all over the country, and sets off on a bus with his bundle of books and papers, certain to draw a full house. It is considered something of an achievement to track him down. Indeed it took some doing, and when subsequently, given his agreement, the production team tried to make an assignment with him, after several attempts they were frustrated. Yet what he has to say represents a very distinctive point of view, and along with the standpoint of the Revd Ray G. Register Jr, it bears recording. They at least mark the intransigeant rocks of faith between which we try to steer our passage.

Yehuhoshua Leibowicz lives in a modest apartment in an ordinary street in west Jerusalem. He has been there for over half a century. He receives his guests in his study, of which the central feature is an enormous flat topped desk, covered with papers. There are bookshelves from floor to ceiling against all the walls. The books are arranged by subjects, carefully classified, regardless of language. On the shelves of philosophy, for instance, volumes of A. J. Ayer, Stuart Hampshire find their places (alphabetically?) between Hebrew tomes and authors like Wittgenstein in German. This is the study of a learned man.

There is one old armchair, which the professor clears of its pile of documents and motions his visitor to sit down. He launches without ceremony into what proves to be an hour-long lecture, pacing up and down behind his desk, arguing with himself all the time. There is a full five minute exordium on some point, and then he turns on himself and says "No!" Then he poses an opposite line of argument, hears himself out, and then proceeds to cope patiently with the familiar objection to his train of thought. Very occasionally he allows a question from his audience, such as he might tolerate from a post-graduate seminar group; but most of the time his flow is impervious to interruption. All that the listener can do is sit and obediently scribble lecture notes.

Between Judaism and Christianity, the argument begins, there can be no dialogue. For Jews and Christians to have conversations about their respective religions is another matter. It might be interesting; it is questionable whether it would be profitable. And why is this? The reason is very clear. Of course Christians are obsessed with Judaism. Judaism is where their faith comes from. But to Judaism, Christianity is irrelevant, a pimple. Historically, of course, it matters a great deal, and I will come to that. But as religion, not at all. Judaism is the revealed religion of the one God, given in the Torah for the Jewish people for all time. Christianity? Christianity is an aberration from it.

You will remember Professor Gilbert Murray's book "Four Stages of Greek Religion". He should have added a fifth – the Christian religion. For the Christian religion is Hellenistic. In the form that it has come down it is largely the invention of Paul. Christians like it that he changed his name from Saul. They do not stop to think why. He changed his name to show that he had renounced his rabbinic past. He identified himself with the Hellenistic world.

Now you have read the later scriptures, which you call the Apocrypha, and you will appreciate that they take our story through the most serious assault on our religion that there has ever been. I hear the objection what about the events of this century, what about this so called holocaust. No, no, the most serious attack on the Jewish religion came at the time of Antiochus Epiphanes, nearly twenty two centuries ago. For then, here in our homeland, they nearly destroyed our religion for ever. They put this blasphemous statue of a man in the Holy of Holies in the Temple. The abomination of desolation, yes. And I will tell you why.

The Jewish religion is theocentric. The Christian religion is anthropocentric, man-centred, not God-centred. It turns our religion upside down. That is the Hellenistic heresy.

From his audience comes the question about archetypes, the parallels between the Old Testament and the New. In particular, is there not some sense in which Abraham's readiness to sacrifice Isaac prefigures the death of Jesus on the cross? Professor Leibowicz deigns to toy with this question.

Then he says, no, they are completely opposite. Abraham was called to show his obedience to God. Whatever Jesus thought he was doing (and how can we know that?) look at what this Paul of yours makes of it. Instead of man being obedient to God he tries to make God obedient to man. God becomes man's slave, his genie if you like. Rub the lamp and wish, and he will do your will. And that is blasphemy. God commands the obedience of his people. It is not for us to seek to command his.

"And what follows?" He fishes amongst his papers and produces a long paper he has written. It is a flimsy carbon copy, in English. "You do not read Hebrew, I think, so you cannot read my new book. But this is the heart of the argument." The paper is a long review-article of the Swiss dramatist Hochhuth's play "The Representative" (*Der Stellvertreter*). It is the play, set during the second world war, examining the question whether Pope Pius XII deliberately turned a blind eye to the Nazi's extermination of the Jews.

"When you have read this," says the Professor, "you will see that I am right. It is of the essence of Christianity to want to destroy Judaism. The survival of Judaism is an affront to Christianity. If the Christian claim is true Judaism should have died out soon after the death of Jesus. The people who wrote the New Testament thought that was already happening. The sack of Jerusalem confirmed it for them. Very soon, they believed there would be no more Jews left. And two thousand years later, where are we?

But of course Christians talk of love. They talk of loving their enemies. They cannot kill all the Jews. After two thousand years they have become sensitive people. It used not to disturb them. In the crusades, they were quite ready to kill all the Muslims. And the Muslims are still here too – but I cannot talk about them now. No, it is the Christians. They have been persecuting the Jews ever since they were in a position to do so. But now they have become sensitive people.

So what are they to do? What is Pope Pius XII to do? What does his religion say? Stop Hitler? Intervene? As a human potentate, he was the one person in Europe who might have had the power to prevent the Nazi extermination programme. But Pope Pius is not only a human being. He is also head of the Catholic Church. And what does his religion tell him to do? It tells him to do nothing. Turn a blind eye. Christians themselves are too nice to do the job themselves. But when Hitler comes, and is ready to do it for them, is he not the instrument of their 'God?"

An implacable upholder of Eretz Israel – the belief that the whole land must be Jewish – we may not have filmed quite such a distinguished eccentric as Professor Leibowicz. Yet the voortrekking spirit is an inescapable element in the Israel of today and that we intended our camera to reflect.

*   *   *

Revd Ray G. Register Jr is the Superintendent Minister of the Southern Baptist Mission in Israel. He has been serving in Nazareth for twenty-seven years. When he first came, it was to start a new mission. Now, around the Galilee he has built up half a dozen separate congregations, and has colleagues from the State sharing his ministry with him. His is the Church whose most famous minister is Dr Billy Graham.

Now aged about 60, and deeply tanned from his long years in the sun, Ray Register has lost nothing of his southern drawl. His comfortable home on a hillside overlooking the old town is a corner of gracious Georgia, and the coffee and cookies his wife produces owe nothing to local cuisine. His avowed mission is to convert the Jews to a living faith in Christ who is their Messiah.

His patient sowing has evidently been rewarded with a considerable harvest. With proper caution, he does not seek to exaggerate the numbers of his converts, but produces a recent annual report with a figure of 2,700. It is not a very large number, he acknowledges, but there are very clear signs that the number of believers is swelling. "Believers" is the term he uses; clearly he finds "Messianic Jews" slightly offensive.

There is on his coffee table a well-thumbed copy of the Authorised Version. In Ray Register's mind, there is no doubt that we are living in the end times. He is not aggressive about it, and perfectly ready to agree that previous generations had a similar conviction. Certainly he does not identify himself with those who from time to time have sought to determine from the pages of scripture the year of the end of the world. "Our saviour warned us against doing that," he said, quite simply, "and we must be faithful to his command."

Altogether there is something impressively steady about him, although with no Professor Leibowicz as his antithesis, in the end we did not include him in the programme. When the majority of concerned Christians in Israel use ecumenism and interfaith dialogues as palliatives for the frailty of their own witness, there is something refreshing in meeting a man whose faith is so unwavering.

"How can anyone call himself a Christian and deny our duty to take the gospel into the world and seek to bring all men to conversion and a living faith in Jesus Christ as their Saviour and Lord?" It seems prudent for his interviewer to say nothing of his own ordained ministry. Argument would be unprofitable.

Ray Register produces a little book that he has written called "Dialogue with Muslims". "Don't worry," he says, "It is not liberal" (as if that were a condemnation). The little book is a few years old, and this is the only copy he has, so there is no chance to read it. A quick glance indicates the line of argument. Yes, certainly the prophet Mohammed was a prophet of God. When he insisted on the oneness of Allah, he was quite right. At that period, in this part of the world, there was much Christian heresy, too easy worship of the saints. Even if the records are scarce, we only have to study what had been going on in the time before the desert prophet appeared. The monophysite Christians, who denied the humanity of Christ, had been cut off from the rest of the Christian world. By their denial of his humanity, they had no argument against those who instead were making too much of the Christian saints. As a result in the oriental world, Christianity had developed into a pantheistic religion. It was against that that Mohammed stood out. He was a reformer as a thousand years later Luther and the others were reformers. The religion of Islam can therefore be seen as an early form of Protestantism. It calls the faithful back to a simple belief in God. As for all that happened after Mohammed, the spread of Islam and the clash with Christendom, that can all be explained by human failing. Under God's providence the time has now come to put matters right, and show the Muslims that they too are inheritors of the kingdom of Christ.

How then did the Baptist mission see its relations with other Christian churches? Again, the patience of Ray Register's response was impressive. Even in New Testament times, there had been failure and weakness in the various churches. Constantly all churches were called back to a more committed presentation of the gospel. In the mercy of Christ many of them were indeed becoming responsive to that call, but the older churches were too much bound up with politics. They were not clearly presenting the pure milk of the gospel.

Political involvement or not, the Baptist Mission is entangled with government requirements through the High School that it runs in Nazareth. While discouraging new ones, Israel's system of secondary education leans heavily upon the large number of Christian schools. They are forbidden by the law of 1978 to proselytise.

Mr Haddad, the deputy headmaster, is a believer, an evangelical Christian, as indeed are most of the teaching staff. The requirement is not absolute. Serving the town of Nazareth, and with Arabic and English as its main languages of instruction, the school does not recruit Jewish pupils. About half the students are Muslim, the rest Christian.

The obvious question is what about religious education. Mr Haddad's answer is equally obvious. "This is a Christian school, and we expect all pupils to attend religious instruction classes in the Christian religion." And do they? To begin with a few Muslims tried to opt out, but the majority of Muslim parents were not prepared to make a fuss. The school, after more than twenty years, had a good reputation in Nazareth. It provided a sound education, in a disciplined setting, at modest fees. There were always more parents wanting to send their children to it than there were places. Then why weren't all the pupils Christians? Again, the answer came as a glimpse of the obvious. In Nazareth there are more Muslims than Christians. And did any of the children become converted as a result of being at the school? Mr Haddad reflected, and remembered the names of one or two who had become believers. Then he said that no, most of them left as they had come simply as Muslims or Christians.

Deeply held convictions, of whatever religion, go against exploratory dialogue with those of other faiths. "There is only one God," Ray Register had said, "and he has revealed himself uniquely in Jesus Christ."

VI

Both doubted angel wings:
   The aged Temple priest,
      A lass in Nazareth

The message that he brings;
   Peace from the lockjawed East
      And end to doom and death.

The old man's speech was gone,
   Unable to believe
His son should be named John;

And that young woman too
   No more could she conceive
With nobody she knew.

They came to songs of praise
   That ritually we clock
But not with their amaze.

All in the Holy Name
   On this eternal rock
Men scramble to lay claim.

When old men lose their tongue
   Reciting prayers by rote
And find themselves struck dumb,

May hope lie with the young
   Who gladly find their note
And may thy kingdom come.

9
To Neve Shalom

Fr Bruno Hussar, OP, is a Jew. This Dominican friar is now in his seventies. In his autobiography, "Quand la nuée s'enlevait" he describes his chequered life. He was born in Egypt, of a Hungarian father and an Italian mother, and spent his boyhood at home in a predominantly Muslim culture. Then in his early teens his father died, and his mother brought him to France. Without any previous religious upbringing, at the age of 17 he had a deep Christian conversion, and announced to his mother than he was called to become a Carthusian monk. Then she told him that she was Jewish, and so therefore was he. Nonetheless, he persisted with his intentions, but was encouraged by his superiors to work in a factory for a while before committing himself.

War came, and within a year the German occupation of Paris, where he now was. Somehow he survived, though never wanting to deny that he was a Jew. After the war he professed as a Dominican, and was shortly afterwards sent to a house of the order in Jaffa. The Jewish Independent State of Israel was struggling to establish itself. The young friar felt sure that his calling was somehow leading him to witness to his dual identity, but it was many years before he could do so. Then in 1959 he was given permission, with a colleague, to found a house in Jerusalem to promote dialogue between Catholics and Jews. La Maison d'Isaac is a scattering of rooms around the flat roof of an old convent building in the heart of West Jerusalem. When he first went there, it was within a few hundred yards of the Jordanian border.

It is still his Jerusalem base. We had already had some contact with him, Jeffrey Milland had been so impressed by hearing him address a meeting in Bristol that he jumped on the train and talked with him all the way to Paddington. So we were certainly expected. Immediately Fr Hussar gives the impression of being a strong man, who knows what he is at. He has a square frame, very upright, and might easily pass for ten years younger than he is. Behind heavy horned rimmed spectacles his brown eyes gaze firmly, but his mouth readily breaks into a smile, and then his eyes twinkle.

He makes light of his past frustrations. The Lord is patient, and it is a matter of learning to be patient too. And look what he has allowed to happen already. Fr Bruno pours lemonade, and warms to the conversation. Of course we are very welcome to film an interview with him, but is it himself or his work that really interests us? Certainly he fits our programme definition "to explore where the three faiths overlap, particularly through the experiences of those who have been touched by more than one of them". He has been touched by all three.

His proudest personal triumph is that he can in Israel legally call himself a Jew. Under Israeli law every citizen has to be registered by race, religion and nationality. The question "Who is a Jew?" has provoked endless argument, and some very significant court cases. To start with it looked as if it should all be straightforward. Anybody who declared himself (or herself) to be Jewish was so. Two legal cases in particular disturbed that simple assumption.

First there was the case of Oscar Rufeisen. He was born in Poland, but he also became a convert to the Catholic faith, and professed as a Carmelite monk. When he sought to register his race as Jewish, it put the cat amongst the pigeons. How could anybody call themselves Jewish by race and Catholic by religion? For the point of including religion and nationality as three separate categories in the Israeli registration of citizenship had been quite different. It had been to protect the susceptibilities of secular Jews. They might want to record their race as Jewish but their religion as none, and that was allowable. But for somebody to register race as Jewish and religion as Roman Catholic was nonsense. So the court ruled against Oscar Rufeisen, Brother Daniel, Ord Carm.

A second classic case raised a different issue. The Shallit family came from Scotland. The husband was Jewish, his wife not; she was nominally a member of the Church of Scotland, and had been so Christened; but both parents were now militantly agnostic. Nonetheless, they wanted to register their children as Jewish. They could not so register them under nationality

(Scottish) or race, since Jewishness is inherited from the mother, and Mrs Shallit is not Jewish. The only way to make the children Jewish was under religion. That meant having them circumcised, and brought under care of the rabbinate. The Shallits objected. They were not religious. Nonetheless, after complex legal argument, the Israeli supreme court ruled that the Shallit boys were Jewish.

Clearly there is room for argument. The law is not clear, and successive governments have shrunk from bringing amending legislation before the Knesset. Thanks to that uncertainty, unlike Brother Daniel, the parallel test case, Fr Bruno Hussar has been able to establish his race as Jewish; and his religion, Roman Catholic. (*Roman* Catholic is no way a put-down; it distinguishes him from being Greek Catholic. Perhaps the document actually says 'Latin', but Fr Hussar did not produce it).

At all events, as he laughingly argued, we could produce him in front of the camera as "Exhibit A". But surely we wanted more than that. Didn't we want Neve Shalom?

Neve Shalom. Yes, indeed we did. For Neve Shalom, Oasis of Peace, of which Fr Bruno is co-founder, is the one place in Israel where Jews and Arabs live together in a commune. It was started in 1972. The original intention was to found a community of people from all the different religions that staked their claim in Israel: Christians through the alphabet from Abyssinian to Zwinglian, Jews, Orthodox, Conservative and Reformed, and Muslims, Shi'ite, Sunni and Sufi; and some in betweens, such as the Druse. To accommodate such a collection Noah would have had to build at outsize ark. As Fr Bruno explained, somewhat ruefully, that original grandiose idea could never have worked. Too many of the folk that he would have liked to attract would simply have not been interested in living there. They were content to live amongst their own relics, as relics. They had been washed up on the rocks of Israel, and become barnacles there. What was the point of trying to prize them off? No, it was just as well, he said (but with a tinge of disappointment in his voice), that after thirteen years, Neve Shalom had come down to basics: Jews and Arabs. Ever since Abraham, they had been the contesting parties for this land. Now, against all odds, half a generation later, there they were still living together. "Get in touch with my co-foundress, Anne de Meignen, and go and have a look."

Improbably, the perspective from which to start is Stanmore, Middlesex. There in a bijou residence live Mr and Mrs Michael Lyons. They are an elderly Jewish couple. Mr Lyons, who retired from business a few years ago, is now chairman of the British Neve Shalom committee.

"It is all because of my sister Coral," he explains. "I said to her, 'you're crazy'. Go and live in Israel, fine. Wouldn't we all like to be able to do that? Live in a kibbutz, if you like. Not very comfortable, but, a very, very nice ideal. But this commune of yours, with Arabs! What do you think Israel is about?"

His sister Coral is Mrs Wesley, or Mrs Pinhas, Aaron. Her husband, answering to either name, depending on the context, is Patriarch in residence at Neve Shalom. Telephone, and the chances are that one or other of them will answer.

Patriarch, perhaps, or figurehead; at least the presence of this elderly couple from England makes Neve Shalom worth the consideration of Stanmore. Otherwise the tenuousness of the commune might cut very little ice.

It stands on an exposed hillside half way between Jerusalem and Tel Aviv, in no-man's land. Down from Jerusalem the road cuts its swathe through a succession of defiles, with rusting armoured vehicles left on the steep banks as a reminder to all who pass. The road debouches into the coastal plain, not far from the Arab town of Latrun. An old tank stands on an iron column as a symbol of victory. Hard across from it is a British mandate police post. At the time of the 1948 struggle, the British put this strategic defence site in the hands of the Arab Legion. Thwarted from approaching the capital along the main road, so guarded, the Israeli forces carved a new track a mile to the South.

The track ran through territory belonging to the ancient Carthusian Abbey of Latrun. This no-man's land is the home of Trappist monks. Neve Shalom is on land loaned from them. Round a bend, and there it is on the skyline. A water-tower is the most prominent landmark, a large metal trough on stilts. Then a mile long dirt track leads up to the place. In March the ruts were still muddy. Winter rains must make it impassable for any vehicle without four wheel drive. It was an immediate contrast with the tarmac of Kfar Hahoresh. The track leads to this little collection of prefabs. There is no prickly pear hedge or other protective fencing to mark the place off. Two weatherbeaten young couples chatting outside the first dwelling extend the familiar greeting: "Shalom" (it could have been "Salaam"). Is it Pinas and Coral we are looking for? No, Anne de Meignen. Ah! (for hers is clearly the name that counts). She lives in the mobile home on the left at the end of the settlement.

There are about twenty buildings altogether, one bigger than the rest, some sort of community gathering place. It does feel like the end of nowhere. A knock on the caravan door, and Anne de Meignen is there with an outstretched hand. She is a trim Frenchwoman (perhaps she is Belgian), in her late fifties perhaps, her brown hair in a neat bob. Yes, Fr Bruno had warned her to expect this visit. There was not much to see, now, was there, but here it was. There were eighteen families permanently living here at the moment, about half of them Jews and half of them Arabs. She could not quite remember how many of the Arabs were Christian, how many Muslims. That was not particularly important. They were mostly fairly young couples, with families of small children. There would not be much point in encouraging single people to come and live here. For they didn't live communally. It wasn't a kibbutz, and it was wrong to think of it as one. A commune, perhaps.

She went on to explain how each family lives in its own house, cooking its own meals and living in its own way. In each family, in principle, one of the spouses has a job somewhere in the neighbourhood, quite often the wives, for at Neve Shalom itself there is a great deal of work for men. They have a few animals, sheep and goats and chickens, and several acres which they farm. It is not self supporting; there is not enough land for them to be able to feed themselves or to grow sufficient cash crops to pay their way. That is why the salaries people earn are important. They don't pool all the money. Families keep more than they need for subsistence; they may not stay forever, and then they will need some money. But they have to pay taxes, and they do pay a proportion of what they earn into the common funds. Even so, Neve Shalom could not have survived thirteen years without outside support. Some money comes from America, quite a large part of it from Britain. Lord Seiff has been very influential in raising funds. Yes, and they do like to have one or two volunteers living with them. They must be prepared to stay at least six months and they must be prepared to learn Hebrew. And not Arabic? Oh, Arabic too, if they care to, but in six months . . . ? Arabic and Hebrew?

Hebrew has to be the common language. In Israel all children have to learn Hebrew at school. Very few Jews know Arabic. In Neve Shalom's own kindergarden the children of course speak both. They seem to have very little difficulty communicating with one another, and they are beginning to grow up more or less bilingual.

"We celebrate all the festivals," Anne de Meignen goes on. "That is when we really come together: Christmas, Passover, Eid-ul-Sukr, yes we keep them all. We find a way of making each of them belong to us all". It is particularly Jewish to make the kitchen the everyday home of religion; all religions find their way in there at festival times.

10
Split Living

Rabbi Pineas Peli lives opposite the Christian Embassy. It is he to whom I owe an apology for being half an hour late for my appointment. No matter, his previous visitor is only just now leaving. Rabbi Peli seems immediately easy to typecast. He is in his late fifties, speaks English with a thick accent, grizzled with rimless spectacles. He is not only a rabbi, with a synagogue and a congregation. He lectures as well, both at the Hebrew University and at the University of Beersheva. His subjects centre round the Jewish contribution to contemporary civilisation.

He was somebody high on Joseph Emmanual's list of recommended contacts. "So you are another of them from British television," is almost his first word of greeting, and asks if I know Ronald Eyre. For Rabbi Peli, in that impressive BBC2 series, "The Long Search", which went out in 1977, had almost a whole programme to himself. He and the producer Ronald Eyre became great friends. Immediately this begins to feel like a wasted visit. What self-respecting producer for the ITV network is going to want to pick up a BBC property. After a polite half hour's conversation, it is time to cut losses and go. At the front door Mrs Peli joins in the farewell handshakes. What a striking woman she is!

It has been a busy enough day already, and three floors down from their apartment there is the little car inviting a free evening. But Mrs Peli! She wasn't in "The Long Search"! Within a couple of minutes their doorbell is ringing again. Is it an umbrella left behind? Or some documents? No, simply an invitation to them both to come out and have dinner. Ah, but they are going to the theatre. It is however time for a little whisky.

Whisky helps arrange the evening's programme. They will be happy to dine as the guests of HTV, and then to take its representative to the theatre with them. So begins a memorable evening, spent at the Khan. The Khan is an old Turkish inn, a relic of one empire that stands opposite the Railway Station, relic of another. It has been beautifully restored. On one side of a courtyard with its fountain and its flowers is the theatre; on the other is the place where you eat (restaurant sounds too formal) it is more than a café; perhaps foyer would do and how English lacks terms for these gradations!

That is where we settle with an hour and a half to go before the play starts. Obviously the undiscovered talent lies with Mrs Peli, Penina. Ten years or so younger than her husband, she has plenty to say for herself. For one thing she is American, so there is not the slightest language difficulty. She is the daughter of an Orthodox rabbi, married to one, and would really like to be one herself. That makes for an improbable opening to the serious conversation. She is unabashed. She has already been leading women's worship in the synagogue. On one occasion she managed to herd a body of men behind the grille which usually screens off the women, to see what it felt like to them. They did not like it, not one little bit. Rooted in her orthodox commitment, she has no expectations that she will get anywhere with her quest during her own lifetime. She has no wish to abandon orthodox Judaism for liberal Judaism, which does allow woman rabbis. "They only play at being Jews," she says. As an orthodox Jew, she is quite certain that the woman rabbinate has to come. "Male and female created he them, in his own image," she quotes. "It is high time we recognised that God is not simply male."

The Pelis are interested to learn of a similar movement in the Church of England. They profess little knowledge of matters Christian, but are well enough informed to appreciate the Church of England's position in the main stream of Christianity. "You are not part of the Protestant churches, and all those sects, are you?" she asks, recalling the various sectarian missions that flourish in Brooklyn, and boldly suggests that the C of E could almost call itself "orthodox", only to Christians that means something else. So she finds new heart in her own calling. If the Church of England can be contemplating women priests, so the orthodox rabbinate should be preparing itself for woman rabbis.

Pineas does not demur. They are obviously very happy together. And then it comes out that for some years now (but since Ronald Eyre was with them, so it can be used) they have been involved in a movement with Christians called "Silent Together". Every so often a group of Jews and Christians meet for a day and have a common retreat. It is not a discussion. It does not claim to be dialogue. Essentially it is silence, and it is prayer. "To the one God, of course". They obviously know much more than they have let on about Christians.

We are now well into our meal, and they begin to express anxiety about taking someone who does not speak the language to a play in Hebrew. Pineas goes to find the author, who is also the producer, and a friend of his anyway. This dapper bow-tied man appears; produces a synopsis of his play in English, which he is delighted to explicate. The title of the play is "Telilah", the name of the heroine. In the course of the play we are able to see her age from adolescence to vast old age. 104, to be precise, and Pineas afterwards invites me to read Psalm 104. Back well up, I point out that the Psalms are very much part of our tradition too. Actually, one brought up in the Protestant numbering of the Psalms has to eat humble pie and appreciate that we are really talking about what Jews, via the Septuagint and most of Christendom, calls Psalm 105. It is one of several that tells the saving history of Israel, ending up "so that they might faithfully keep his statutes: and faithfully obey his laws O praise the Lord". The essential plot of the play is that the author, an Everyman figure, is in search of his true faith. He pursues it, in the person of Telilah, through various episodes. Temptations abound, and he is led into them, but over all hover a black chorus, easily identified as the Chassidic presence, which constantly prevents him from reaching his grail. Under the weight of this chorus, and the lures of the world, Telilah grows virginally older, and at the climax of the play, made up to show her great age, succumbs to death under a pile of dead leaves. But then there is a transformation scene, hinting that the two might after all live afresh and happily ever after.

It was a surrealist theme, and a surrealist production. With the author/producer's help, it was extraordinarily easy to follow; there in those converted stables of the Khan an audience of a couple of hundred was kept spellbound, and the spell easily held a spectator who understood not a word.

Over coffee, afterwards, in the Peli's flat, a place in the

programme was pledged for them both. They have each since, separately, been to London, and for once high-flown words about lasting friendship may yet be made good. Shalom!

By crow it must be just about a mile to the foothills of the Mount of Olives. For all the contact that might be conceivable between the Pelis and the Mshashas it could just as well be a million miles. Ouissema Mshasha is a Muslim eternal student. But for one more episode in that chain of misunderstanding, bad timing and embarrassment that bedevil the making of documentary television, he would without question have contributed to the series. He assured the production team that he would make good his undertaking to appear; and did not.

Yet there, an undulation or two away from the Khan, and the afternoon following that performance, the Mshashas were celebrating. It was the naming of another grandson in the extended family; one more nephew (perhaps cousin) for Ouissema. At any rate it was his father's home, and without a shade of awkwardness Ouissema encouraged his English driver to plough through the swarm of kids playing in the yard and park outside the family home.

The celebrations were well under way. That morning, being Friday, the seven year old infant had already been taken to the Imam and named; presumably circumcised, as Ishmael was (it seemed indelicate to enquire). In any case, whatever other ritual the Imam had performed, he had done the thing that mattered and sacrificed two kids. Now was the moment to enjoy them.

Mr Mshashsa (père) has for many years earned his living as a driver at a Roman Catholic school in Jerusalem, and educated his children there. His single-storey home clambers up the steep slopes with extension after extension. It is just as well. He is a prolific patriarch. There were, Ouissema reckoned, at least one hundred and twenty members of the family present for this feast: uncles, aunts, cousins, wives, nephews, nieces, – it did not do to be too particular. This Arab feast did nothing to resolve one of the nice questions of scriptural scholarship whether the brothers and sisters of Jesus were really cousins (nephews, nieces, even uncles and aunts; or even step brothers). Ouissema remained engagingly vague about current Muslim attitudes towards polygamy. It was a clan.

One social custom remained intact. The men kept apart from

the women. There was gaggle and gossip in the kitchen. In the salon the men were assembled. There were a dozen or more, sitting as in a dentist's waiting room, on divans against the walls. Mr Mshashsa held court in what was clearly his chosen corner. There was coffee. So long as the English guest's arrival was a matter of common interest, Mr Mshashsa interlocuted in careful French, and translated the essentials to his kin. Interest flagged. But then an adolescent girl crept in with a towel, to serve as a tablecloth, and another followed with an enormous helping of rice and choice portions from that kid. A third, a little girl, wide eyed, arrived with what was obviously the family silver, a knife and fork. When in Rome . . . but this was east Jerusalem. The barest diplomatic good manners insisted that this feast be enjoyed, as if had already been by the other hundred and twenty members of the family, by eating with one's fingers. The chunks of kid are easy enough. To be a novice at eating gooey rice between the thumb and two fingers needs private practice. It must be only the right hand. To use the unclean left hand to assist in a ritual of this delicacy would offend against every one of the seven pillars of wisdom. Alas, the British mandate has gone, and the memory of El Aurenz, that figure of Lawrence of Arabia, is as tarnished here as his later biographers have made it in England. How else is one to exhibit appreciation generally except by consuming this horrendous mound in silence? It is not an easy thing to do, at three o'clock in the afternoon, when one has unwarily already lunched.

Six-, seven- eight-year old urchins peer constantly through the door at this improbable participant in their family feast. With the mound of food still formidable, there is only one thing for it. There is a particular family variation of hide-and-seek called Cockiolly. "Cockiolly" sounds as if it needs no translation into Arabic, and the rules can be explained by mime. Soon twenty or thirty kids are soon scurrying around Mr Mshashas domain, shouting "Rescue" and "Danger" as if they had been playing it all their lives. Ouissema clearly reckons it is time to abstract his embarrassingly familiar guest. He has agreed to act as guide to Jericho, twenty miles down the road. Almost immediately he starts pouring out his heart. There he is, still a student, but well past his middle twenties, and unmarried. He has been a student, at the Hebrew University, one of the precious eleven per cent that the authorities like to claim (no apartheid here). He is still one, but he has to support himself. What has broken his heart is his aborted romance with a Christian girl that he met there.

It wasn't surprising. His father works in a convent school. He had been a pupil there. He was very attracted to the Christian religion. But he is a Muslim. It was a high school for girls, but the nuns took little boys. After that he had gone to another school. But he had a childhood sweetheart, and they kept in touch. He grew up, she grew up. They were still sweethearts. They studied together. They were in love. He was prepared to become a Christian. Certainly Jesus was a great prophet, son of Mary. She was a good girl. Maybe it was her family, not his. His father would not tell him. From whichever side it was, family pressure had been intense. They had considered eloping together but where could they go? She could not afford to be cut off from her family. He could not afford to support her; and he was a Muslim. Now his family had resolved matters. Within a few months he was to marry a cousin from Amman. And had he met her? Once, he thought, but it might have been her sister.

In Jericho Ouissema led the way to sites that the tourists miss. In any case the sun had fallen behind the Judaean hills. Twilight is short, and the official sites had closed. Instead Ouissema pointed out what really establishes Jericho's claim to be the oldest city in the world: water. With almost the pride of possession he led the way to a secret spring, from which through carefully dyked canals water flows to irrigate the allotments. Ouissema took pride in demonstrating the system of sluices. Lift this gate, and your patch is watered; close that, and another's is dry. But be watchful.

In Jericho's broad, warm avenues, the streets in March are lush with local produce. Oranges, lemons, grapefruit abound. There are also liquats, a sort of cherry plum, of which an unwary traveller buys a kilo. They are extremely bitter.

We returned by a different route. Ouissema was not at all uncomfortable at driving up the northern bypass which skirts the Arab villages of Bethphage and Bethany and brings the traveller safely to the suburbs of Jerusalem. For, here, on the back slopes of Mount Scopus, and under the shadow of the tower of the Hebrew University, he took immense pride in displaying the plot of land that he had bought to build himself his family home. He had saved up enough money to buy the plot. He had no money left to build a house, and no means (as Nazareth had taught) of raising a mortgage. No problem! He had twelve cousins (at least!) who would help him build a house. One was a bricklayer, one was a carpenter, one was an electrician, one was a plumber, no problem. In two months' time his home would be built, and then he could summon his bride from Amman and marry her. Within a year he would easily have earned enough money to repay his relations; and they did not ask for interest. In Ouissema's calculations, usury has no place. That is for Jews.

For all his professed claim to be interested in interfaith relations, it remains extraordinary to think that Ouissema's family lives only a mile or so away from the Pelis' delightful flat.

★　★　★

Half way between them lives Mrs Anna Grace Vester Lind. "In at the Damascus Gate, turn left, and keep turning left, and count a hundred and twenty steps. Ask for the Americans." Mrs Lind is an Anglo American dowager, scion of a prominent Quaker family. Her brother owns and runs the American Colony, the cream of hotels in east Jerusalem. The house where she presides in ageless widowhood has been in her family for over a hundred years. One anticipates a retinue, but she unbars and opens the front door herself, and, carefully bolting it behind her, ushers her visitor across a court into her reception room. In Jerusalem society she holds a peculiar place. She is widely known and respected, has the ear of the Mayor, and as Quaker is immune from at least internecine religious politics.

So she leads the way up a couple more flights of winding stairs, meticulously bolting each door behind her as she goes. The stairs are narrow and uneven, but for all her years, this silver haired grande dame takes them in her stride. "There!" she says triumphantly, as we reach the roof, and there, from its highest vantage point, lies the old city and a whole panorama beyond. Seigneurially she points out monuments familiar and unfamiliar, notes that the way to tell an Arab from an Israeli home is by seeing which direction its television aerial faces: the Arab ones pick up Amman.

She has kept her choicest treat till last. From the eastern edge of her roof we are looking sixty feet down on to an open space. It has a little hut, and a football pitch, with goalposts, where a dozen boys are practising. The houses you can tell by the aerials; there is no way of telling these boys. This is the Spafford Childrens Playground, the one amenity in Jerusalem designed to be used by anyone, irrespective of race, nationality or religion; and so used. The only effective limitation is age. After about the age of fourteen, youngsters simply do not come any more; but by then they should have learned something about living in harmony and peace.

For those who follow the western Christian calendar, the following weekend brings Palm Sunday. That afternoon there is a procession, down from Bethphage on the Mount of Olives, through Gethsemane and across the brook Kidron up the hill and into the old city by St Stephen's gate. Led by two bimbashis with their pacesticks, a relic of Ottoman rule, the long train makes its way, with a desultory singing of hymns and high good humour. Behind a posse of priests, there is party after party of uniformed schoolgirls. Every single member of one group wears in her beret a Solidarnosc badge. This sudden mass display of support for fellow Christians in Poland is surprising and touching, until it transpires that their school is run by Polish nuns. In this city Solidarnosc has overtones. Fifty years ago twenty per cent of the members of the Polish *Sejm* (parliament) were Jewish. Now, we are constantly reminded, Poland is ninety five per cent Catholic. Most of those Jewish MP's and those they represented perished in the extermination camps. Those who survived form the core of the ruling power in Jerusalem. They are not the beneficiaries of Solidarnosc.

Patiently and peacefully, under military surveillance, the procession crowds through the narrow gate into the old city. Suddenly there is disturbance. Somebody is barging their way through the crowd, two fisted forearms flailing a passage. One blow strikes your intrepid reporter's ribs, and he turns round indignantly to confront the perpetrator. It is Anna Grace Vester Lind. She is quite unabashed, and explains that "You have to fight to get peace in this place".

11
A Footprint of Hope

Sister Maria Goldstein is American, and a Roman Catholic nun. With a name like that, she can't help being Jewish. She is a secretary of the Hope Interfaith Society.

Like everyone else, she takes some tracking down. The house where she lives is easy enough to locate. It is only five minutes walk down the road towards Bethlehem from Tantur. Time after time the garden gate is locked, and the bell does not work. Nor does the telephone. It has been suspended. The thing to look for is her blue VW Beetle. When that is parked outside it means that she is at home.

There at last she is, all bustle and welcome, dispatching a younger sister to make coffee. Indomitable, she talks of her trials and her labours. Certainly in Tantur itself she is handled with caution. Time was when she more or less lived on the premises, but even after her own house was established, she regularly came beetling up the drive to make full use of the office facilities. Politely at first, and then very much more firmly, she was told that she was no longer welcome, except when invited.

All this, and much more of the same, she rides without any trace of bitterness. "Mary, dear," she says to her returning acolyte, "you may pour the coffee," and continues with her flow. It is never going to be easy to break through all the barriers of mistrust, but that is her calling and she must get on and do it. Her group meets every Friday morning, at the Pontifical Institute and there is a hearty invitation to attend.

Friday comes. The green grille of the Pontifical Institute bars the way into one more imposing pile of late nineteenth century ecclesiastical architecture. "Hope" serves as the password, and there in a salon twenty people are already gathered. An extremely good looking man, in a yarmulka, is holding forth on a passage from Jeremiah. He is Rabbi David Rosen, former Chief Rabbi of Ireland, before that in South Africa, and frightfully British. His audience is middle aged and more, and respectable. There are two Jewish couples, at home with their Hebrew texts. One Scots lady prominent in the class turns out to be the widow of an Armenian, and most of the others are western Christians. There is reputed to be a Muslim in the group, and, yes, there tucked in a corner is Ouissema. Sister Maria sits at the rabbi's right, jollying proceedings along. Eventually, with Passover coming, we are distributed English copies of the Halakah, in order to study its liturgy.

One less than dedicated student finds his attention readily distracted. For there, in the appendices at the back (front) of the book are two surprisingly familiar readings. There is a version of the "House that Jack built" and there is a (non Christian) version of "Green Grow the Rushes, O". A better researcher would have made a note of the Talmudic alternatives to four for the gospel makers, twelve for the twelve apostles and eleven for the eleven who went to heaven. The ten commandments and all those stars are common ground.

The seminar ran its decorous course for an hour or so, and then came an invitation to join the core-group for lunch. They would be planning their interfaith Holy meal to take place on Sunday evening. Lunch was at Stella Maris, another great Roman Catholic pile at the apex of the city, now serving as a comfortable hotel. There was no question of Friday abstinence, or any hint that Sister Maria is short of funds. There are half a dozen members of the core-group, best seen as Sister Maria's sounding-board. She was overjoyed at the prospect of television. The question was what could be done. The conversation worked its way round to the notion of an outdoor interfaith seder, to be held on Ascension Day in the Mosque of the Ascension.

The Mosque of the Ascension is one of the most moving old shrines in Jerusalem, for some reason not much on the tourist track. The old minaret is dwarfed by the spires of two Christian churches. It stands in an octagonal space, whose walls are embellished with marble pillars where the crusaders tethered their steeds. Quite possible. In the centre is a small domed chapel, lit by a skylight directly over the rock that it enshrines. For on this slab of rock the faithful can see the outline of a footprint. It is the footprint of Christ's ascension. Byzantine pilgrims poured mud into its mould, and when it hardened bore it home as a precious relic. Scepticism is too easy. This unassuming sanctuary does not have to strain after holiness, and there is nobody to fuss the devout. Outside an old man sells rosaries and postcards, but plies his trade very gently. A small notice reminds visitors that this shrine belongs to the Muslims, but in the name of Allah, the all-merciful, they are happy to let Christians pray here. It is a very good place.

And it would be a very good place to end our programme. For above all the jumbled strata of religious rock that is Jerusalem, it is open to the sky, and hints at a whisper of peace. The mark of Christ's parting footprint encourages the attempt.

There are complications. There are always complications. For a start, Ascension Day is only a Christian festival. There would be something inappropriate for the Hope Interfaith group planning a seder for that festival. It would look too much, reckons Sister Maria, like a Christian takeover. Round the core-group there are nods of assent. After all, she reasons, Ascension Day more than any other is the triumph of the Christian year. It proclaims Christ as king of the universe. Nervously the soft spoken Melchite woman teacher from Bethlehem Silvamia enquires whether this matters. Her husband, Fuad, hitherto silent, agrees with her. Isn't the whole point of the interfaith group to proclaim the oneness of God? Would not Ascension Day demonstrate that, but still be open to other interpretations? After all, only the very credulous want to take the footprint of Christ possessively as their own symbol of proof. It invites more. It is a mark, undoubtedly, that has been revered by pilgrims since even before there were any Muslims. Yet it is they who guard the shrine, they who are moved to open it to Christians. At Easter Christians claim Christ for themselves. For forty days they claim him as risen for those who have eyes of faith. On Ascension Day they let him go, saying that they can no longer keep him tied down. That day, if any, is the one when the interfaith group should be able to celebrate their first glimpse of a common faith.

It is a moving argument, but the group as a whole is still uneasy. We cannot expect to show a glimpse, is Sister Maria's argument. The best that we can hope for is a glimpse of a glimpse. In the end the group reaches a compromise, to have an interfaith seder there on that day, and be filmed, but to make it for pentecost. Pentecost is after all a Jewish as well as a Christian festival. This year, happily, they coincide. Moreover, by another happy chance, this year it falls just before the beginning of Ramadan, and that makes it a Muslim feast too.

The next set of complications concerns permission. The Muslims may let Christian pilgrims visit the Mosque of the Ascension without difficulty. It is another matter getting permission to film there. That will require HTV obtaining the necessary permit. Today is Friday, the Muslims holy day, and all their religious offices are shut. During the course of the weekend it should be possible to get permission, and then we can confirm all the arrangements when we meet for the interfaith seder this coming Sunday evening.

It calls for another visit to the Temple Mount. At eight o'clock on Sunday morning the gateway to it is already open. A janitor seeks to bar access. "Too early, no visitors". The name of an official, and a mime of rubber stamping and camerawork gain begrudged access. The janitor puts two fingers in his mouth and whistles to attract the attention of his mate two hundred yards along the colonnade. An arm beckons. At this next sentry post there are already half a dozen custodians on duty for the day. The offices are not yet manned, and it is time for breakfast. So seven of us sit cross-legged in a circle to dip the sop. Large round loaves of bread appear, and a big bowl of hummus sprinkled with parsley. Bread is broken and passed from hand to hand. The bowl is in the middle for all to share. So at his last meal Judas shared, but without the tiny cups of sticky coffee that are the seal of Arab hospitality. English cigarettes continue to be an acceptable token of gratitude. It is a lingering breakfast, and they play dice. Not for the first time comes the reminder that seeking permission in Jerusalem is a time consuming question, and could Jesus' trial and crucifixion have really been arranged so rapidly?

In due course one of them leads the way upstairs to the office of the all-important official. He is not in the best of tempers, and he has no printed forms to authorise permission to film. Ahmed, the young janitor, waits patiently alongside. He has clearly taken on responsibility for the success of this mission, and is glad to serve as interpreter. Eventually the effendi tears out a page from an exercise book, and makes the best of a ball-point pen for his calligraphy. A row or rubber stamps stand expectantly to hand. He pens his way through a good dozen lines, and then asks Ahmed a question. When is it that we want to film? Seven week's time. He snorts, and tears the paper away. We should not be wasting his precious time now. We are to come again then.

Ahmed evidently feels his diplomatic standing is at risk. Now he leads the way back into the precinct of the Temple Mosque and across to another set of offices by the side of the Al Aqsa mosque. There he knocks timilly on a door and we are in the presence of Mohammed Said el-Jamal. His is the sufi personage that radiates reverence. He has open before him the Koran, and his lips move as he fingers his way through the familiar suras. With good grace he closes the holy volume and attends to his interruption.

"There is no god but god, and Moses is his prophet (blessed be his name) and Jesus is his prophet (blessed be his name) and Mohammed is his prophet (blessed be his name)." In this elevated vein he discources for some ten minutes. It is the frailty of man, and his disobedience to god, that has created three religions, and allowed them to continue in enmity for so many hundreds of years. Mystics of each tradition must give themselves to earnest prayer that the three traditions be open for one another and learn to find how to worship the one true god. Perhaps God in his mercy is already sending another prophet through whom he will reconcile his previous revelations.

He hears gladly of the proposal to film an interfaith seder at the Mosque of the Ascension. With his help there should be no difficulty. He lives on the Mount of Olives. There is no need to write down his address. Every child in the street up there knows who he is and where he lives. He is here at the Al Aqsa mosque in the mornings, but in the afternoons from three o'clock he is back up there. Then he rises and gives his parting benediction: "Go well in the name of God".

These joyful tidings need to be reported to Sister Maria and her co-religionists at this evening's interfaith seder. For the past couple of days she and her two sisters in their little convent have been making preparations for it. It is due to start "after the Palm Sunday procession". But her gate is locked. There is nobody about. In the drizzle a ballpoint pen refuses to write. All that can be left (for it is only hours till the plane leaves for London) is the barest of scribbled notes: "Sorry Shalom CM".

It was stupid not to have realised that the seder was taking place in the salon of the Pontifical Institute. In Jerusalem and the parts round about it the few fragile seeds of hope are very easily mislaid. Goodness knows what concatenation of trivial circumstance eventually put paid to the interfaith seder on the Mosque of the Ascension that was to end "One God . . . Three Gods?" on such an upbeat. Sister Maria Goldstein still has brave words to say.

Shelley Elkayam
Poem from Song of the Architect

YES INDEED I'LL ANSWER GOD

And this is the judgement.
I will ever be what I now am inscribing letters in light.
A small letter as a sign in a crown of light.
Peace unto the crown.
Peace unto the King and the Queen and peace, peace unto the escort.

Don't take it to heart.
Wind hovers over the deep
and space is laid out between the lines from sentence
to sentence like
chess: black and white.
Like on a park bench: a sitting king's falling.
A parable, my beloved readers:
the garden's song
and the architect's checkmate.

And whoever wants to come to the garden –
arise and enter.

Bless this breach.
Peace to Yeshurun.
Welcome, Lord's favor.
And Bless the Name, naturally, day by day in Mahane Yehuda.

All kidding aside.
Believe me, the Gates of Grace are already open.
Right now, this minute, today and forever,
and this song a witness between you and I
alive this instant, all, like they say,
with love and awe and completion.

Please don't worry.
For right before your very eyes what's written
is written. And that's a fact.

To everything there is a season and this is the time
since that's how song goes –
a pillar of fire:
intransitory.

And whatever is distinct has intention –
in other words, perfection within perfection.
Whatever you decide,
I'm with you.

As for me,
I took it upon myself for the sake of the song so in
deed I'll come back to God.
And I gave my word
to grow to the scent of a blossom of light.
To be kindled by the right aroma.
To be
Amen.

Truly, simply, with love.

And whoever is bound
and finds himself in the garden, finds himself
in the garden: sing to him:
Come, my pleasantly tied,
unlace yourself in the palm
of my hand.

Now I return to
the man among you who is fine and tender.
Now, since I was reminded, I remember now.
My blood my soul my heart and will are one.
One – regardless.
You are one.
One now.

Enough.
This is judgement.
And I take the verdict upon myself
at its word.

Therefore, for the sake of the liberty you gained
all ceremonies of the covenant
are memorial.
In remembrance, of course.
Like a garden bell. Accordingly:
I forgive my father for doing things without questioning my desire.
Look, after all, the ledger's open.
Ceremonial testaments inscribed in the body.
A man and his covenant
carved in his form.

Accept this, take it upon yourself
and look at the voice
how
suddenly the body's stone.
The body suddenly ape.
                      Ape.
The body suddenly blossoms.
At once the body's at the Gates of Grace
and someone utters – live, now
and who
ever wishes to enter the garden
arise
in fragrance
whoever among you is a man of fine and tender
scent.

*Translated from Hebrew by Ammiel Alcalay, Jerusalem 1985.

Postscript

For once postscript is a strictly accurate title. The filming has been done. Gillian Reynolds has made her interviews and they have generally gone well. There were one or two disappointments, one or two items that ended on the cutting room floor. Besides the contributions from Cairo, there were other people to be found in Jerusalem with significant things to say. Now, between editing and transmission, how does the theme of the programme stand up to the original conception? In the end that must be for the viewers to judge, and if the series does anything to prompt reflection of how the three montheistic religions – Judaism, Christianity and Islam – relate to one another, we shall have achieved our intention. We were not setting out to make an adult education series in comparative religion. We sought to express the relations between the three religions "particularly through the experiences of those who have been touched by more than one of them."

Print can at least attempt what is far more difficult on screen: it can try to bring some sort of order to the ideas on which we touch.

Religions are languages that offer those who are native in them a structure for expression and belief. Any mature language contains all that its user needs to shape his thinking and form his beliefs. Yet as any translator knows, it needs more than a word-for-word dictionary to turn one language into another. Thought forms vary, and what makes moving sense on one language in another sounds over-blown or stilted.

Moreover, however, complete a language may be, it has gaps. French has to lend other languages the vocabulary of eating out. English reciprocates with its richness of sporting terms. Italian provides the world with the phraseology of music. The French are gastronomes, the British pioneer outdoor games, and the Italians have a musical language.

For a start then it would not be surprising to find that each of the three – Judaism, Christianity and Islam – however complete in itself, has particularly developed certain religious sensibilities. So, for instance, all the language of sin that Christianity has made its own is a direct inheritance from the Hebrew Bible. On the other hand, the central concept of the love of God is peculiar to Christianity, and Judaism has not adopted it. For in Christian Europe, at least, Judaism's survival has hung on not assimilating. The central ideas of the Muslim religion are the otherness of God and the need for man to submit to his will. Islam, meaning submission, freely and from the first acknowledges its debt to its two predecessors. In concentrating on God's otherness and the need to submit, it from the beginning staked out its distinctiveness.

For all their incompleteness, and need to borrow from one another, the guardians of language are reluctant to let them mix. The Academic Française fights its battle against "Franglais". Esperanto, the language of hope, has celebrated the centenary of its invention, and claims its thousands of speakers; but it has not really caught on. Similarly, the golden dome of the Ba'hai temple in Haifa stands as a pitiable witness to the hundred and fifty year old attempt to mix the religions of the world. They do not mix that easily.

Since the historic Edinburgh Conference of 1910, the ecumenical movement amongst Christians has made unimaginable strides. Allowing that for the moment its progress seems to be slower, it is not surprising that some Christian pioneers have largely led the way into interfaith dialogue. There is danger in seeing too close a parallel between the two forms of activity.

Between the three religions (and the various expressions of them) the gaps are very much greater. It is as if the countries of Scandinavia, having made considerable, but not complete, progress towards common understanding, instead bent their energies to a lingua franca for Europe. The differences are far more profound.

Thanks to the Americans, English has supplanted French as the prime language of negotiation for western Europe. Only a person whose first language is English realises what a poor shadow international English is for the tongue of Shakespeare. International English serves a valuable purpose, as did *koine* Greek in New Testament times. That in turn was a bastard of classical Greek, and who dreamt in it?

For an authentic language, like an authentic religion, must be rich and real enough to inspire dreams. Accordingly those for whom religion seems to mean most deny the possibility of exchange. Professor Leibowicz has his peers in Christianity and in Islam: in effect, you worship your god in your way, I will worship mine in his. There is no room for converse.

The difference between a Leibowicz and his peers is that they have the urge to convert the unbeliever. Yusuf Islam and Ray Register and their like feel the need to preach conversion as part of their fabric of belief. Christianity and Islam are both missionary religions. Judaism has a different sense of mission: simply to be obedient, survive, and so witness to the one unnameable god.

All three of them necessarily frown upon those who indulge in interfaith dialogue. It is an activity, they impeccably reason, only undertaken by those who do not really believe in their own god. They are religious charlatans.

To this obduracy there is a very clear parallel in the way that conservative evangelical Christians regard the ecumenical movement. In their eyes, true believers are one in the Lord. The canon of true belief is to be able to give testimony to a experience of conversion that has led the individual to acknowledge Jesus Christ as personal Lord and Saviour. Anyone who hesitates to give voice plainly cannot really claim to be a Christian. As for denominational differences, they do not matter very much. The New Testament church clearly had "differences of administration". For these to persist may witness to human failing, but they are of secondary importance.

Against that, those who think that the ecumenical movement is important claim that the divisions of Christians are a scandal: even in its original Greek sense of a stumbling-block to faith. How, they argue, can Christians be good missionaries if they sweep their divisions under the carpet?

Unlike comparative religion, which has been for two centuries or so an academic discipline, interfaith dialogue is in its infancy. So far the distinctions that mark Christians differences of standpoint have not yet become clear. What is the interfaith equivalent of the conservative evangelical test of conversion? It sounds as if it ought to be a simple belief in God. Or what is the equivalent of ecumenical anxiety over the scandal of divisions?

It can only be that in this shrinking world, Jews, Christians and Muslims ought to be ashamed of their inherited divisions, and seek to reconcile them. These two thoughts bear pursuing a little further.

First, what would be the test of faith? It would have to be some sort of profession of belief, that would boil down to something like this:

"I believe in the one God, maker, sustainer and judge of the world. I believe in his constant call for his obedience to his will, but also in his lasting readiness to forgive us our failures. I believe that there is more to human life than our senses show, and that God wants us to enjoy him for ever."

Any attempt to devise a common creed is foolish. Creeds are part of the Christian lumber; they have no place in Judaism or Islam. Such dilutions lead only to vanity. There is nothing to live by here, nothing to hold. This level of generality belongs better to the everyday world of the United Nations Charter and the Declaration of Human Rights. It is in this runny mud that Ba'hai and others attempts to be syncretistic and mix religion invariably flounder.

For a while a creed looks like a positive document of belief; it is not really that. Its business is to define boundaries. Anybody who cannot give assent to it is out. The traditional concern of religions has been to determine who belongs and who does not.

Instead of demanding creed, Jews and Muslims have a much simpler sign: circumcision. There is no question of a baby boy expressing assent; there is no doubt that he belongs to the tribe. Traditional Christianity has a similar sign: infant baptism. Again it does not seek assent; it claims to be an indelible sign.

Neither circumcision nor infant baptism ensures commitment to the religion. Circumcision has a better chance: it is a daily reminder of membership. The sign of the cross in baptism leaves no visible tattoo. That is why evangelical Christians demand a conversion experience as the only proof of belonging. To their question "When did you become a Christian?" the answer "When I was baptised as a baby" will not do.

To Jews the problem of commitment comes up in a different way. "Once (sealed as) a Jew, always a Jew" is a comforting truism, but what about those who assimilate? With no comparable physical sign for women, Jews perpetuate themselves by their insistence that Jewishness comes through the mother. So the sign that holds a woman bound is the knowledge that, willy-nilly, her children will be Jewish. Even so, over the centuries, there has been a constant drain of the collective lifeblood of Jewry as individuals marry out of the religion, and in a generation or two any claim to be Jewish has gone. Their eqivalent passion to the evangelical Christian's insistence upon conversion is therefore that their children marry Jews.

For Judaism and Christianity are both strictly monogamous. Practice may lapse, but the principle that a man should only have one wife remains very strong in both religions. Moses permitted divorce "for the hardness of your hearts" but there are Jews who like to maintain that, whatever its religious meaning, the very act of circumcising a male infant makes for marital fidelity. The physical assault cuts into the protesting infant an instinct that the enjoyment of sex is inseparable from the pain and responsibility of generating new life.

That rationalisation of a primitive custom cannot apply in Islam, where traditionally men can marry more than one woman at a time, and divorce them quite easily. Women do not enjoy the same freedom. Interfaith dialogue between the three religions may abort simply because of the Muslim attitude to women. In orthodox Judaism (till Pineas Peli has her way) in the synagogue women are kept behind the grille. In Islam, they take no part in the prayers of the Mosque.

Evangelical christianity focusses attention on commitment. Ecumenical Christianity sees a main priority in "faith and order".

Is there in this area any scope for interfaith dialogue? The orders are so totally different. The analogy between religions and languages may bear taking a step further. For all the movement towards a federal Europe, the notion of member states giving up their separate sovereignty is well beyond practical discussion. Short of abandoning their identity altogether, how could the Grand Duchy of Luxembourg and its three neighbours (let alone the rest of the twelve) make one country.

Between the Jewish, Christian and Muslim religions (and their branches) the differences of order run every bit as deep. As a religion, Jewry is not hierarchical. It is congregational, and a synagogue of at least twelve bar-mitzvah'd males is autonomous. The rabbinate constantly seeks to ensure order, but claims no powers over the faithful, except to say who belongs and who does not. By contrast, most Christians belong to a hierarchical church. Councils and synods may seek to make it more republican, but the dominant structure is monarchic. The further Christians move from that centre, the more they become sects.

Shi'ite tradition has something of a similar awe for the word of the Chief Iman. In the Aga Khan, the Ismaelis have a leader of heroic stature. In Islam Sunni Muslims do not; rather like orthodox Jewry, they stay intact (and in the majority) by the constant interpretation of tradition.

Even to hint at the differences of order between and within the three religions is to show that it would be preposterous for interfaith dialogue to develop itself into a constitutional commission. Conceivably the time for that could come, just as between diverse Christian traditions there are patient committees working away and reporting. It is a very distant conception.

The roads for exploration seem blocked. The routes that ecumenical dialogue between Christians has taken in this century appear to offer no guidance, yet, for interfaith enquiry. At best it is a matter of sketching out the terrain and inviting others to follow. Is there any other way round?

One possible form of activity is to talk about the three gods. Of course, there is only one god, said all the sympathetic people whom we met. His worshippers see three very different faces. Do they conform to any sort of identikit? Christians immediately stall the discussion by calling their god "God". His full name is "God the Father, God the Son, and God the Holy Spirit" but it shortens with disarming ease to "God". Neither the Jews nor the Muslims do this.

To the Jews the central revelation of the Torah, the first five books of the Bible is the name of God: I AM THAT I AM. It is a revelation so sacred that in practice they never dare name him. Christians have taken over Jehovah – Jahweh – and bandy the name around. Generally, though, they stick to "God". Whether "Allah" is simply the Arabic for "God" is a nice question. The consensus of scholarship suggests that in the time of Mohammed (blessed be his name) "Allah" was the chief of a vague pantheon of gods, and what the prophet did was to discard the rest and emphasise the uniqueness of Allah. No doubt the generality of Muslims hearing the muezzin cry five times daily "Allah Akbar" translate it in their minds as "God is great". In that case they are stuck with the same problem as the Christians. They are better at saving themselves from it. Just as Jews get round the awful silence of the holy name by using a host of periphrases – the Lord of Hosts, the keeper of Israel, and so on and so on, so Muslims have their ninety-nine names to fall back on. For all that terrifying oneness, there is a prism that breaks it up into a less dazzling spectrum.

Christianity borrows from the Hebrew scriptures a similar tendency: "Lord of Lords and God of Gods – Hallelujah!" Isaiah and Handel are only one obvious source of the names. But still Christianity spoils the possibility of interfaith dialogue by its unquestioning assumption that the name of god is "God". For names matter. Naming the creatures was Adam's first task. To be able to name somebody is to be able to know them. To address God as "God" is like addressing everybody as "man" (or "woman"). It hardly makes for intimacy.

Every day Christians say "hallowed be thy name" and forget what it is. To Jesus it was "Abba" – "Dad". Tongue-loosened Christians will indeed begin their prayers with "Father" (which is more formal), or even "Heavenly father"; but then they dare not quite think of that as God's name (which they pray to be hallowed) since they have to allow that Jesus and the Holy Spirit are both somehow equally God. So the prayers that chattily start "Father . . ." are only part of it, when Christians are particularly reminding themselves of God's care, concern and power. When it is God's forgiveness they are after the prayers addressing Jesus Christ. Rather more awkwardly and self-consciously, prayers inviting guidance are made to the Holy Spirit. God the Holy Spirit sounds much more impersonal; and for all the present fashion which seeks to see the Holy Spirit as the feminine side of god, in Greek it is a neuter word. The one thing Christians dare not do is to start their prayers, as Jesus did, with "Dad", but then Jesus was not a Christian. Somewhere below Christian verbosity lies a trace of that Jewish instinct which dare not say God's name because it is too holy. And for them, as much as for Jews and Muslims, God is one.

Christians do not believe in three gods, and Trinity is not arithmetical formula. The point of the doctrine, which took four centuries to evolve in its static form, is to save Christianity from the charge of making God man-centred. The Holy Spirit is the Father's makeweight against the manhood of Jesus.

It is tempting to speculate how it would have been if Athanasius had not stood against the world, and if Arius had prevailed. Arius saw Jesus as God dressed up as a man, like a prince in a fairy tale. So he preserved the essential otherness of God. If Arius had won, would Islam then have arisen? Might we not by now have learned to have restored the identity of Abba and of J*HW*H? To Professor Leibowicz, Christianity is the fifth stage of Greek religion, essentially man-centred. Religion in his view, demands man learning to be obedient to god, who is one, and other than man. He is different from Allah chiefly in that he concentrates his attention on his peculiar people the Jews, and expects them to go on witnessing to him. He is, in Martin Buber's presentation, one pole in the eternal I-thou relationship; it is up to each of us to work out whether God is "I" or "Thou". Just as two of the figures in that sculpture can be either Moses or Jesus, so this question remains open-ended.

Twenty years ago Christianity weathered death-of-God theology. Now consensus of thought and experience recognises that God is very much alive, whatever we may be. The footprint in the rock of the Mosque of the Ascension may be beckoning the adherents of all three religions to pray together that they may somehow share in the gift of that transformation.

Christians cling to Trinity as obstinately as Jews cling to the land of Israel. "In the name of the Father, the Son and the Holy Spirit" is the password of Christian orthodoxy. Unitarianism, and the religion of Swedenborg, are the dreary relics of a half-hearted Christian attempt to go along with the deism of the age of reason. If Christians want now to engage in serious dialogue with their Jewish and Muslim cousins, they need to be prepared to test the hoary doctrine of the Trinity without demoting Jesus, for the idea that God revealed himself as human still invites exploration. That exploration has to begin by encounting the blasphemy that Leibowicz articulates and that Judaism and Islam both identify in their rejection of Christianity. They are both stuck with God as other and appalled at Christianity's claim to make him one of us. If Christianity had died out soon like its contemporary Mithraism, Islam might still have arisen as a move to make Judaism Universal. J*HW*H and Allah have a very strong family rememblance. That is not how it happened. Though there is a school of thought that sees the ancient Hebrews at home in Arabia, and so the direct forebears of Islam, clearly the prophet Mohammed, six centuries after Jesus, had a revelation that went against the prevailing Christian religion.

In the centuries to come, Christianity and Islam could too easily resume their embattled opposition with frontiers over the globe, Western Christianity, after a lull of five hundred years, becomes sensitive to Islam as a threat. The time for dialogue is now.